MENSA MATH

Derrick Niederman, Adam Hart-Davis & Raymond Blum

Illustrated by Jeff Sinclair

**OFFICIAL MENSA
PUZZLE BOOK**

Main Street
A division of Sterling Publishing Co., Inc.
New York

Library of Congress Cataloging-in-Publication Data Available

2 4 6 8 10 9 7 5 3 1

This book is excerpted from the following Sterling titles:
The Little Giant® Book of Math Puzzles,
© 2000 and written by Derrick Niederman
Amazing Math Puzzles, © 1998 and written by Adam Hart-Davis
Math Tricks, Puzzles, & Games, © 1994 and written by Raymond Blum,
Illustrations © 1994 Jeff Sinclair

Published by Sterling Publishing Co., Inc.
387 Park Avenue South, New York, NY 10016
© 2004 by Sterling Publishing Company Inc.
Distributed in Canada by Sterling Publishing
c/o Canadian Manda Group, One Atlantic Avenue, Suite 105
Toronto, Ontario, Canada M6K 3E7
Distributed in Great Britain and Europe by Chris Lloyd at Orca Book
Services, Stanley House, Fleets Lane, Poole BH15 3AJ, England
Distributed in Australia by Capricorn Link (Australia) Pty. Ltd.
P.O. Box 704, Windsor, NSW 2756, Australia

Printed in United States of America
All rights reserved

ISBN 1-4027-1638-9

CONTENTS

THINK TANK PUZZLES

EASIER BY THE DOZEN

Place the numbers from 1 to 12 as follows:

The odd numbers go in the triangle. The even numbers go in the circle. The numbers that are divisible by three go in the square.

How will this look?

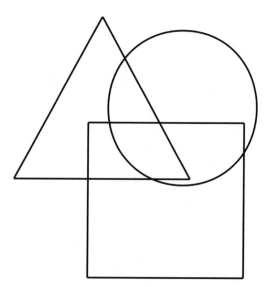

MAGIC CIRCLE

The numbers 1 through 9 are arranged in a circle. Can you divide the numbers into three groups—not changing the order—so that the sum of the numbers in each group is the same?

EGGS-ACTLY

If it takes three and a half minutes to boil an egg, how long does it take to boil four eggs? Be careful!

(Magic Circle) Hint First figure out the sum of all nine numbers. Divide that sum by 3, and you have the sum of each of the three smaller groups.

(Eggs-actly) Hint When the problem asked you to be careful, that's a warning to watch out for a trick!

JUST CHECKING

Five kids sit down to play some games of checkers. If each one of the five kids plays one game with each of the others, what is the total number of games played?

Hint: Remember, if Ted plays against Jennifer, Jennifer is also playing against Ted! If you like, you can use A, B, C, D, and E for the kids, and then list all the one-on-one match-ups.

THE ONE AND ONLY

Believe it or not, there is only one number whose letters are in alphabetical order. Can you find it?

LETTER PERFECT

Rearrange the letters in the phrase ELEVEN PLUS TWO to create a new phrase with the same meaning!

(The One and Only) Hint Trial and error will get you there! Note that the answer has more than one digit, which is sort of a clue right there. And you should be able to rule out two-digit numbers in bunches.

(Letter Perfect) Hint The new phrase also consists of three words, and one of them is left unchanged!

COUNTDOWN

How many rectangles can
you find in this diagram?

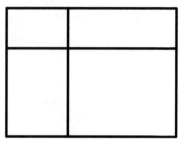

SQUARE ROUTE

Four dots are arranged in a square.
Starting at the upper left dot, draw
three straight lines, each line going
through one or more dots, so that
you end up where you started.
Every dot should have a line going
through it.

(Square Route) Hint All three lines go beyond the boundary of
the square.

(Countdown) Hint Remember, a rectangle is any four-sided
figure where the sides meet each other at 90 degree angles.

NO HONOR AMONG THEIVES

A valuable jewel was stolen from the Emerald City of Oz. Naturally, suspicion was placed on the three non-human visitors—the Scarecrow, the Tin Man, and the Cowardly Lion. They went to trial in front of the famous Wizard of Oz.

At their trial, the Scarecrow claimed that the Tin Man was innocent. The Tin Man claimed that the Cowardly Lion was innocent. As for the Cowardly Lion, he mumbled something that no one could understand.

YOUR HONOR, PEOPLE WHO STEAL HAVE NO *BRAINS!!*

If an innocent person never lies and a thief always lies, which if any of the three suspects is guilty?

Hint Assume first that the Scarecrow is guilty, then proceed to the other two suspects, one at a time. See if you come across anything that contradicts your assumption of guilt.

CIRCULAR REASONING

Only one of the four lines in the diagram below divides the circle into two equal parts. Can you find that line?

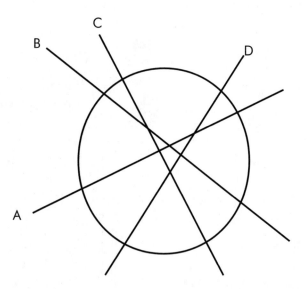

Hint In order for a line to divide the circle into two equal parts, that line must go through the center of the circle.

CONNECT THE DOTS

Can you place ten dots on a page using just five lines of four dots apiece?

PICKUP STICKS

If you count out the matchsticks below, you'll see that the statement works out just fine. But can you rearrange the matchsticks so that the statement is still true and you don't need to do any counting?

$$||||||||||||||||||||||||||||| = 29$$

(Connect the Dots) **Hint** The answer is actually a very familiar shape. If you can figure this one out, you're a real star!

(Pickup Sticks) **Hint** Twenty-nine is an unusual number. No other number would work in its place in this problem. Note, for example, that it doesn't have an "O" in it!

LONG DIVISION

Professor Mathman went to the blackboard and demonstrated to his astonished class that one-half of eight was equal to three! What did the professor do?

Hint Professor Mathman was being tricky. It's easier to do the problem if you think in terms of the number 8 rather than the word "eight."

WHEN IN ROME

Was the previous problem too easy? If so, try to come up with a way of proving that one-half of nine equals four.

NUMBER PATH

Place the numbers 1 through 20 in the grid below so that they form a continuous chain. In other words, starting with 1, you must be able to get to 2 by going left, right, up, or down—but never diagonally—and so on, all the way to 20. Just make sure that the positions of 3, 7, 10, and 16 are just as you see them. There is only one solution. Can you find it?

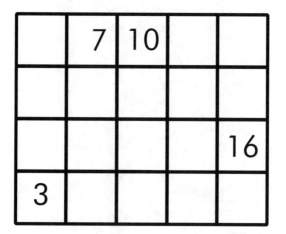

SEEING IS BELIEVING?

If you continued drawing the line at the bottom left of the diagram below, and kept going up, which line would you meet up with, A or B?

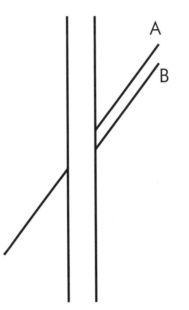

DIAMOND IN THE ROUGH

Of the four suits that make up a deck of cards, only the diamonds are symmetrical, in that a diamond—unlike a club, a heart, or a spade—looks the same whether it is rightside-up or upside-down.

However, one of the 13 diamond cards is different when you turn it upside-down. Without checking any decks of cards you may have lying around, can you name that one non-symmetrical diamond?

Hint The idea is to visualize how the diamonds are put on the cards. The only hint you'll need is that there are never three diamonds in a row *across* the card, although for the higher numbers there are certainly three or more diamonds in a row going *down* the card.

THREE'S A CHARM

There is an inexpensive item that can be purchased for less than a U.S. dollar. You could buy it with four standard U.S. coins. If you wanted to buy two of these items, you'd need at least six coins. However, if you bought three, you'd only need two coins. How much does the item cost?

Recall that you have only five U.S. coins to work with: A penny (one cent), a nickel (five cents), a dime (ten cents), a quarter (twenty-five cents), and a half-dollar (fifty cents).

Hint It's probably easiest to look at the combinations of two coins. What combinations of two coins produce a number that is divisible by 3? For example, a quarter plus a penny equals 26 cents, which is not divisible by 3, so this combination can be ruled out. On the other hand, a nickel plus a penny equals 6 cents, which is divisible by 3 but isn't nearly big enough to satisfy the problem! One you get the right combination of two coins, you can work backward to get the rest of the answer.

WHO IS THE LIAR?

Four friends—Andrew, Barbara, Cindy, and Daniel—
were shown a number. Here's what they had to say
about that number:

>Andrew: It has two digits
>Barbara: It goes evenly into 150
>Cindy: It is not 150
>Daniel: It is divisible by 25

It turns out that one (and only one) of the four friends
is lying. Which one is it?

NO FOOLIN'

In the year 2000, April 1 (called April Fool's Day in
many parts of the world) took place on a Saturday. On
what day was April 1, 1999? What about April 1, 2001?

(No Foolin') **Hint** There are 365 days in most years, almost
precisely 52 weeks. "Almost," that is. The fact that 365 is not
evenly divisible by 7 is at the heart of the problem.

(Who Is the Liar?) **Hint** First assume that Andrew is lying,
and see if it is possible for Barbara, Cindy, and Daniel to all be
telling the truth. Then do the same for the other three. In only
one case will there be only one liar.

SQUARE DANCE

First count up the number of squares in the figure below. Can you remove just four line segments to cut the total number of squares in half?

Don't leave any segments "hanging." Every segment must be part of at least one square.

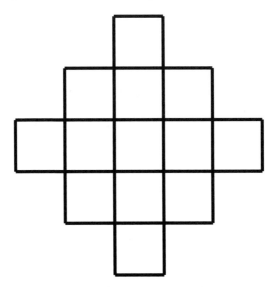

PLEASE FENCE ME IN

Suppose you had a long stretch of fencing with which to make a nice big playpen for your new puppy Sam. If you wanted to give Sam the biggest possible area to roam around in, what shape should the fence be?

Hint All that you need for this one is common sense. You're not being asked to come up with proof that one shape is best. Now that would be tougher!

PRIME TIME

A number is called "prime" if its only factors are itself and 1. (Although 1 is not considered a prime number.) The first ten prime numbers are hidden in the square below. Can you find them?

We suggest taking a pencil and filling in every square that contains a prime number.

32	16	24	33	45	28	54
40	23	2	11	5	19	12
14	36	10	55	17	34	49
6	50	38	13	22	51	20
21	35	3	46	27	18	39
9	29	48	15	4	52	26
55	44	25	8	42	30	1

Hint At first glance, there are only nine prime numbers in the diagram. But if you follow the directions carefully, you might find the tenth one.

PIECES OF EIGHT

An octagon is an eight-sided figure. A stop sign is perhaps the most familiar example of a "regular" octagon, in which all eight sides have the same length. Inside the regular octagon below, we have drawn three "diagonals"—lines connecting two of the extreme points. How many diagonals are there in all?

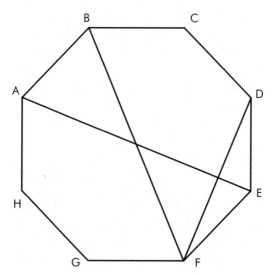

Hint Be sure not to "double-count" the diagonals. The diagonal joining A to E is the same as the diagonal joining E to A.

ON THE TRAIL

One of the numbers below becomes a common
English word when converted into Roman numerals.
Which one?

38	54	626
1,009	2,376	3,128

SPREADING THE WORD

Suppose you want to make copies of pages 12, 19, 30,
31, and 47 of your pocket dictionary. If it costs a dime
to make one copy, how many dimes will you need?

numbers.
never stop?! Just make sure to take a close look at the page
(Spreading the Word) Hint Another trick question—will they

50, C = 100, D = 500, and M = 1,000.
(On the Trail) Hint Remember that I = 1, V = 5, X = 10, L =

THE BIG INNING OF THE END

On Sunday, May 7, 2000, the Houston Astros defeated the Los Angeles Dodgers 14-8, in ten innings. Where was the game played—in Houston or in L.A.?

FROM START TO FINISH

Imagine that the diagram to the right represents city blocks. The idea is to walk from point S to point F, and

(The Big Inning of the End) Hint) In baseball, the home team bats last.

of course you can only walk along the lines. The entire trip is five blocks long. In how many different ways can you make the trip?

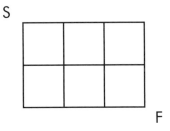

HOW BIG?

In the figure below, we have drawn lines from each corner of a square to the midpoint of one of the opposite sides. How big is the smaller square in the middle—as compared to the original square?

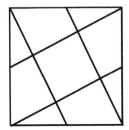

(How Big?) Hint Try putting together the shapes that surround the central square.

(From Start to Finish) Hint Let A stand for across and D for down. How many different combinations can you make of 3 As and 2 Ds? (For example, AAADD corresponds to traveling from the Start to the Finish along the outermost route. There are many other routes.)

THE BIRTHDAY SURPRISE

A math professor was lecturing his students on a remarkable fact in the world of probabilities. The professor noted that there were 23 students in the class, which meant that the likelihood that some two people in the room shared a birthday was 50 percent!

The professor expected the students to be surprised—most people figure that you'd need many more people before you'd have a 50% chance of a shared birthday. Yet the class wasn't surprised at all. In fact, one student claimed that the professor had miscalculated, and that the likelihood of a shared birthday in the room was in fact much greater than 50%.

What had the professor overlooked?

Hint: For this particular class, the likelihood of a shared birthday was almost 100%!

NOT JUST ANY WORD WILL DO

Little Ashley was trying to remember her father's phone number at the office: 269-1000. He explained to her that you could spell the word "any" by using letters that correspond to the 2, 6, and 9 on the dial.

But Ashley wanted a better word than ANY, so she stared at the dial. She eventually found five other words that could be formed using the letters from 269. Can you find those five words?

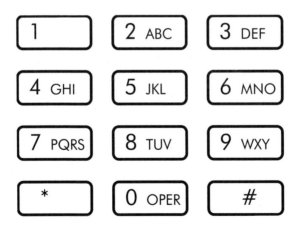

Hint Four of the words are familiar nouns, while the fifth word is an adjective that may not be quite as familiar.

THE RUN-OFF

In a 10-kilometer race, Alex beat Burt by 20 meters and Carl by 40 meters. If Burt and Carl were to run a 10-K race, and Burt were to give Carl a 20-meter head start, who would probably win?

STAYING IN SHAPE

The figure below shows one way to join four squares at the edges and make a solid shape. How many different shapes can be created out of four squares? (Two shapes are not considered different if one can simply be rotated to produce the other.)

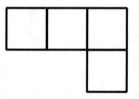

(Staying in Shape) **Hint** Pencil and paper are really required for this one.

(The Run-Off) **Hint** It's a trick question. The trick is to see that the race between Burt and Carl will not be a tie.

MIRROR TIME

Below is the digital display of a clock reading four minutes after four. As you can see, the hour and minute figures are the same. It takes one hour and one minute before you see this pattern again—at 5:05.

What is the shortest possible time between two different readings of this same type?

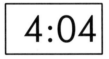

Hint There are twelve such times during each twelve-hour span. Going from 1:01 to 2:02 takes one hour and one minute; same for going from 2:02 to 3:03. But there is one occasion when the time gets shorter.

WHOSE SIDE ARE YOU ON?

Jeanne and Cindy play two sets of tennis. Jeanne starts on the sunny side (top) and Cindy starts on the shady side (bottom). According to the rules of the game, players switch sides after every odd game in each set. Assuming that Jeanne won the match, 6-3, 6-4, which side were the players on when the final point was played?

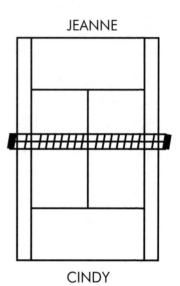

JEANNE

CINDY

Hint For those of you who have never played tennis, all you need to know is that a typical tennis match is the best two-out-of-three sets, and to win a set you must be the first player to win six games. Some matches involve tiebreakers for close sets, but tiebreakers weren't necessary for this particular match. Remember, in this match Jeanne and Cindy would have switched sides after the first set.

ONE OF A KIND

To write out the number "fifteen," you need seven letters. When you write out "ten," three letters are required. There is one and only one number for which the number of letters needed is the same as the number itself! Can you find that number?

WIN ONE FOR THE DIPPER

Can you draw three straight lines in the diagram at right so that each star of the Big Dipper lies in its own separate region within the rectangle?

(One of a Kind) Hint Fortunately, the number you're looking for isn't all that big. But you suspected that, right?

(Win One for the Dipper) Hint Use a ruler and use pencil! Also, you might want to look at the page from an angle, just to make sure that you can draw a line through certain spaces.

GOING CRACKERS

A cracker company isn't pleased when it finds out the results of a survey it has taken. According to the survey, although customers would rather have a cracker than have nothing at all, those same customers would prefer peanuts to anything else!

A junior employee at the company decides that this is his big chance for a promotion. He claims to his boss that what the survey really said was that customers prefer crackers to peanuts. How in the world could he come to that conclusion?

Hint: The secret to this one is in the wording. You have to find something that is both "better" than peanuts and "worse" than crackers. Sometimes there's nothing tougher than a good logic problem!

FIVE EASY PIECES

In the diagram at right, the big square is divided into four equal parts. Can you divide a square into five equal parts?

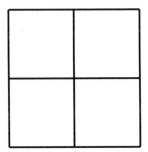

IT'S IN THE BAG

One bag contains three red marbles and two blue marbles. A second bag contains two red marbles and one blue marble. If you could pick only one marble from one of the bags, which one would you choose if you wanted to give yourself the best possible chance to pick a red marble?

(Five Easy Pieces) Hint Don't forget the title. Whatever you do, you don't want to make this one harder than it really is.

(It's in the Bag) Hint The idea is to calculate the two probabilities as fractions, then to compare those fractions.

SWITCHING SIDES

Start with nine dots arranged in a square. The diagram below shows how to join some of the dots to form a figure with five sides. What is the greatest number of sides that a figure formed in this way can have? Remember, the figure must be closed—no loose edges permitted.

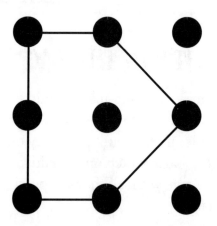

THE MISSING SHEKEL

A farmer in ancient Transylvania took his rutabagas to market each week. His standard price was three rutabagas for a shekel. On an average week, he sold 30 rutabagas and came home with 10 shekels.

One week, he agreed to sell the rutabagas grown by his neighbor, who wasn't feeling well enough to make the trip into town. The only surprise was that the neighbor's preferred price was two rutabagas for a shekel. When the neighbor sold 30 rutabagas, he came home with 15 shekels.

The farmer decided that the only fair thing to do was to sell the combined crop at the rate of five rutabagas for two shekels. But when he added up his money after selling both his crop and his neighbor's crop, he had only 24 shekels, not the 25 he was expecting.

What happened to the missing shekel?

Hint Is the price of five rutabagas for two shekels as fair as it looks?

WHAT DO THEY PLAY?

Stacy, Alex, and Meredith play golf, chess, and soccer, but not necessarily in that order. Can you use the following clues to figure out who plays which?

A: Stacy gave the soccer player a ride to the last game.

B: The chess player said that Stacy drives too fast.

C: Meredith went to the prom with the chess player's brother.

Hint: This problem is solved by ruling out rather than ruling in. And keep in mind that Meredith didn't go to the prom with her own brother!

CLASS DISMISSED

Suppose school starts promptly at 9:00 a.m. If each period lasts 40 minutes and there are 5 minutes between periods, when will the fourth period end?

QUARTER HORSES

Two horses live on a large piece of land shaped like a quarter-circle. The horses' owner wants to give each horse its separate space by building a fence on the property, but it is important that the two horses have the same space in which to run around. Below are three ways in which a straight fence can be installed to divide the area precisely in two. Which fence is the shortest? Which is the longest?

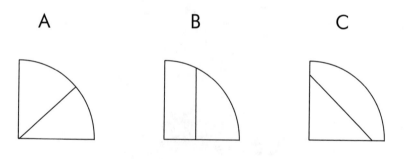

A   B   C

Hint The simplest thing to do is to compare each length to the radius of the circle. The radius of the circle is the length of either of the straight lines that form the quarter-circle.

AND THEN THERE WAS ONE

Begin by crossing out the letter N. Now go around the circle, counter-clockwise, crossing out *EVERY OTHER* letter you come across. If you keep going in this fashion, what will be the last letter? Remember, once you have crossed out a letter, you do not count that letter as you go around the circle a second or third time.

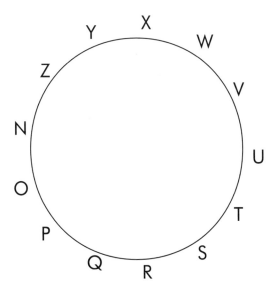

Hint Just keep going, and don't forget that once a letter has been crossed out, it has disappeared for the purposes of this puzzle. And use pencil!

DOES GOLD GLITTER?

"All that glitters is not gold," the teacher said.

"You mean that gold isn't the only thing that glitters?" Tracy asked.

"No," Sean interrupted, before the teacher could answer. "He means that gold doesn't glitter."

Well, who's right?

Hint There's no right or wrong here, but you are encouraged to try and see things from Sean's point of view.

FOUR OF A KIND

Divide the figure to the right
into four identical pieces.

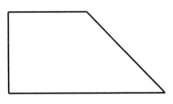

HEX-A-GONE

Drawing just three lines, can you
transform the hexagon to a cube?

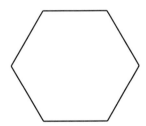

(Four of a Kind) Hint If you divide the figure as shown below
in the following way, you can see that the total area equals six
small squares (five are intact, and the other two halves combine
to make the sixth one). So if you want to divide this figure into
four equal pieces, the size of each piece must be 6 1/44 = 1 1 1/42
small squares. Go from there!

(Hex-a-Gone) Hint Try separating the hexagon into three
diamond-shaped pieces and see what happens!

X MARKS THE SPOT

Can you place five more X's in the grid so that every row and column has an even number of X's in it?

					X
	X	X			
	X				
	X				
X				X	
			X	X	

ALL IN BLACK AND WHITE

Start with the number of seasons in a year. Multiply by the number of planets in the solar system. Add the number of cards in a complete deck—without the jokers.

What you end up with is another special number, but one that isn't quite as well known as the three numbers you've just seen. Do you know what makes the final number special?

(X Marks the Spot) Hint By definition, each row and column must have either 2 or 4 X's in it.

(All in Black and White) Hint A deck of cards—without the jokers—contains four suits of 13 cards apiece, for a total of 52 cards. The rest is up to you!

SWEET SIXTEEN

Of the fifteen snowmen pictured here, no two are alike: Some have white eyes, others have black eyes; some are smiling, others are frowning; some have eyebrows, others do not; finally, some have noses, and others do not.

Because there are four different features, the total possible number of snowmen equals 2 x 2 x 2 x 2 = 16. Can you draw the missing snowman?

Hint Note that precisely eight of the sixteen total snowmen must have any one of the facial features described in the puzzle. So if you see that eight of the 15 original snowmen do not have eyebrows, the 16th *must* have eyebrows! And so on.

MAGIC TRIANGLE

On the left is a "magic" triangle. What makes it magic is that the numbers on each of the three sides of the triangle add up to 12. Can you place the numbers from 1 through 6 in the blank triangle on the right in such a way that each of the three sides of the new triangle adds up to 10?

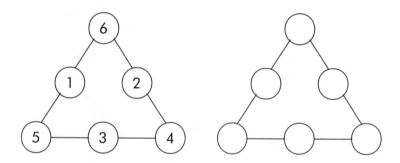

Hint The key to the puzzle is figuring out the corner numbers. In the example given, the sum of each leg was as big as possible (12), so you had to use the three biggest numbers in the corners, where they would count twice. To get 10, you have to make a change.

AN UPDATED CLASSIC

Sixteen matchsticks have been arranged to form a backward "L." See if you can add eight matches to form a region separated into four identical smaller regions. It's an old problem, but not everyone realizes that there are two completely different ways of solving it. Can you find one of these solutions?

Hint One of the solutions takes place totally inside the "L" shape, and the other one ventures outside.

EIGHT IS ENOUGH

If you start with a 3 x 3 arrangement of dots, there are 8 different-shaped triangles that can be drawn by connecting 3 of those dots. To get you started, two of those 8 triangles have been drawn in below. Can you find the other 6?

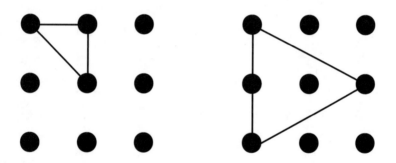

WHERE'S WALDO?

Waldo is in the fourth grade. In Waldo's class, everyone sits in the same chair every day, and there are the same number of kids in every row. One day a substitute teacher came in and asked where Waldo was sitting. He was too shy to answer, so several of his classmates answered for him:

Maria said, "Waldo sits in the third row."
Jerry said, "Waldo sits in the fourth row from the back."
Alice said, "Waldo sits in the second seat from the right."
Oliver said, "Waldo sits in the fourth seat from the left."

How many students are in the class?

Hint Drawing a diagram is one way to get the solution. Don't forget that there is an equal number of students in each row—without that, you couldn't figure out the total number of students.

THE CHRISTMAS CAROLERS

A group of Christmas carolers came across a neighborhood of five houses, as shown below. It had just snowed, and the carolers wanted to create a path with their footsteps joining every pair of houses. They also wanted to visit every house on their journey. They didn't mind visiting a house more than once, but their rules didn't permit walking on a path they had already been on.

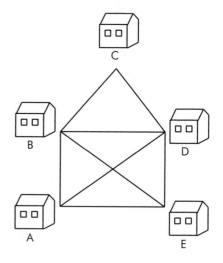

Suppose they start caroling at the Andersons—house A. Where will their journey end?

FOREVER YOUNG

Heather was born in the middle of winter in 1966. In April of 2006 she claimed to be only 39 years old. How can this be?

ALL IN THE FAMILY

Each of the four Strickland brothers has a sister. Altogether, how many kids are in the family?

(All in the Family) Hint The puzzle states that each of the brothers has a sister. It doesn't say that each of the brothers has a sister of his own sister.

(Forever Young) Hint Another trick question. We never said where Heather lives.

SQUARING THE CIRCLE

In the diagram, a circle is nested inside a large square, then a smaller square is tilted and nested inside the circle. How big is the tilted square in relation to the larger one?

Hint Puzzles like these are often solved by drawing extra lines so that you can see the answer without any calculations. Try drawing the two diagonals of the tilted square and see if that helps!

TOO CLOSE FOR COMFORT

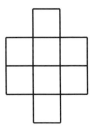

See if you can place the numbers 1 through 8 into the boxes at left so that no two consecutive numbers are touching— either horizontally, vertically, or diagonally!

PRIME TERRITORY

We know that a prime number is a number whose only factors are itself and 1. We also know that there is only one even prime number—and that is 2. Now for the puzzle, which is to find a three-digit number with the following properties:

A) Each of the three digits is a prime number, and

B) Each of those digits divides evenly into the three-digit number.

so, in what position would it have to go?

prime are 2, 3, 5, and 7. Is 5 in the number we're looking for. If **(Prime Territory) Hint** The only single-digit numbers that are

sure that the numbers in the two middle boxes are far apart! keep close numbers far apart, you might want to start by making hold the key to the solution. Since the idea of the puzzle is to **(Too Close for Comfort) Hint** The two boxes in the middle

STAY OUT OF MY PATH!

The idea of this puzzle is to connect the four pairs of similar squares: the gray with the gray, the X mark with the X mark, and so on. But can you connect the four pairs so that none of the four pathways crosses any of the others?

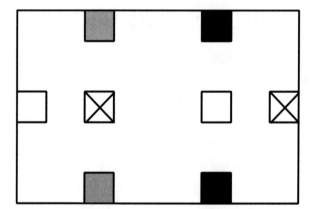

Hint Two of the routes are fairly direct, but the other two are long and windy. Try to use space wisely. Don't crowd yourself out. It's okay for two paths to run alongside each other for a stretch, but they must not cross.

HUNDRED'S PLACE

Suppose the "skyscraper" pattern below kept going and going. Would the number 100 belong to a short column, a medium column, or a tall column? Can you figure this out without writing out all the numbers in between?

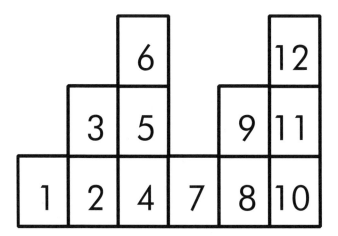

Hint Note that the top number in each of the tall columns is a multiple of 6. If you use this pattern, you can see what happens around the number 100 without writing out all the numbers.

OCCUPATIONAL HAZARDS

Three men—Mr. Baker, Mr. Carpenter, and Mr. Potter—
work as a baker, a carpenter, and a potter, but none of
the three men has a job that matches his name. Also,
each of the three men has hired the son of one of the
other men as an assistant; again, though, none of the
three sons works in a profession that matches his name.

If Mr. Carpenter is not a potter, what does young Mr.
Baker do?

Hint You should be able to figure out Mr. Carpenter's job based
on the information in the puzzle. Once you have his job, you can
figure out his son's job, and so forth.

STRAIGHTENING IT OUT

There are seven pieces, labeled A through G, in the crooked shape to the left below.

There are eight pieces in the rectangle at the right. One piece has been added from the crooked shape and some have been turned over. Can you identify the added piece?

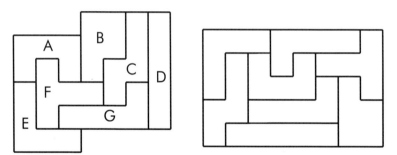

Hint Looking at the right-hand rectangle, each time you see a piece from the crooked shape, check off both pieces. That should lead you to the added piece.

NUMBER GHOST

The idea behind the following puzzle is to start with the number 2681 and choose a number that begins with the same digit that 2681 ends with, which is 1. Once you find it you need to locate another number, one that starts with the same number that your new number ended with—kind of like a game of Ghost, but with numbers. Keep going in this way so that you form a chain of numbers. The chain stops when you find a number whose last digit is 2—which happens to be the first digit of 2681. Can you make a chain that is five numbers, including the initial 2681, from among those below?

2681	1247	8499	5023	4387
5687	2309	7829	1235	6885
9123	6403	1569	4862	1298
5342	5706	8914	3190	6283

Hint Remember that the chain must have at least five different numbers in it!

LAST TRAIN TO CLARKSVILLE

Brian, Amy, and Stephanie are waiting at the train station. Each of the three is waiting for a different train. When they check the station clock, they realize that Amy is going to have to wait twice as long for her train as Brian will for his, while Stephanie will have to wait twice as long as Amy!

What time is it?

DESTINATION	TRACK	DEPARTURE
NEWBURGH	3	4:48
SPRINGFIELD	7	4:57
CLARKSVILLE	4	5:15

Hint The first step is to figure out how much time goes by between the departures of the various trains. There is only one possibility for the current time.

CROSSING THE BRIDGE

In the game of bridge, a standard deck of 52 playing cards is dealt among four people. The cards held by a particular player are called that player's "hand." Players assign a value to their hands by counting 4 points for an ace, 3 points for a king, 2 points for a queen, and 1 point for a jack. Sorry, but you don't get points for any other card.

Suppose that you are dealt a hand with one ace, three 7's, two 5's, and two 4's. Even without looking at your other cards, what is the greatest number of points you could possibly have in your hand?

Hint Remember, a deck of cards consists of four suits of 13 cards apiece. There are only four aces, and the same holds for kings, queens, and jacks.

SHOWING YOUR AGE

For their twentieth wedding anniversary, Richard and Sylvia had a party for several of their best friends. Things were going along just fine until one of their friends asked the happy couple who was older! Here's what they had to say.

Richard: "I am older than my wife."

Sylvia: "I am younger than my husband."

That might have been the end of it, but one of the guests knew that at least one member of the couple was lying. Well, who is older, Richard or Sylvia?

Hint See what happens if you assume that precisely one of the two—Richard or Sylvia—isn't telling the truth.

TEST PATTERNS

Can you locate a copy of the 3 x 3 square below in the 9 x 9 square on the next page?

 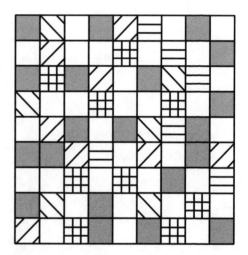

Hint Just try and focus on the diagram without going dizzy! One strategy is to look for a couple of particular squares in the smaller pattern, and see where they come up again within the larger pattern. In other words, don't try to memorize the entire 3 x 3 pattern!

COOKIE MONSTER

A bag contains three cookies, and each of them is different: one chocolate chip, one oatmeal raisin, and one sugar cookie. Elmo reaches in and picks one cookie, then Peter does the same. Who has the better chance of ending up with the sugar cookie—Elmo, who went first, or Peter, who went second?

Hint As with many puzzles, you can solve this one by using numbers or common sense or both. What if there were a third person? What would that third person's chances be of ending up with the sugar cookie?

THE END IS IN SIGHT

Starting with the "T" at the top of the diagram and moving from one diamond shape to another *TOUCHING* diamond shape, in how many ways can you spell out "THE END?"

GLOVES GALORE!

Gloria's favorite colors are pink and yellow. She has socks in those colors, of course, but she *really* likes gloves!

In her glove drawer, there are six pairs of pink gloves and six pairs of yellow gloves, but like Sam's socks, the gloves are all mixed up. In complete darkness, how many gloves does Gloria have to take from the drawer in order to be sure she gets one pair? She doesn't mind whether it's a pink or yellow pair.

THE WOLF, THE GOAT, AND THE CABBAGE

You are traveling through difficult country, taking with you a wolf, a goat, and a cabbage. All during the trip the wolf wants to eat the goat, and the goat wants to eat the cabbage, and you have to be careful to prevent either calamity.

You come to a river and find a boat which can take you across, but it's so small that you can take only one passenger at a time—either the wolf, or the goat, or the cabbage.

You must never leave the wolf alone with the goat, nor the goat alone with the cabbage.

So how can you get them all across the river?

NINE COINS

Wendy got into trouble in her math class. She was sorting out money she planned to spend after school, and accidentally dropped nine coins on the floor. They fell with such a clatter that the teacher was angry at the disturbance and told Wendy to remain at her desk after school until she could arrange all nine coins on the desktop in at least six rows with three coins in each row.

Can you do it?

Wendy did. In fact she did even better. She arranged her nine coins in no less than *ten* rows, with three in each row! Her teacher was quite impressed.

Can you make ten rows?

EIGHT COINS

Here's a really neat puzzle that you can use to baffle your friends. Once you learn the secret, it's easy, but if you don't know the secret, the puzzle is quite hard. Still, you just might luck into it, so why not try your hand before you look at the answer.

First you have to make a line of 8 coins on the table, like this:

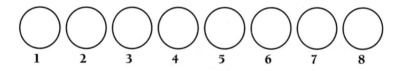

Pick one coin, jump it over two others, and put it on top of the third. The challenge is to finish with four piles of two coins after only four moves.

Hint It's simply a matter of knowing which move to make right at the start.

ODD BALLS

Lucky you! You have nine tennis balls and four shopping bags.

Your challenge is to put all the balls in the bags in such a way that there is an odd number of balls in each bag? That is, each bag must contain 1, 3, 5, 7, or 9 balls.

Can it be done?

TRICKY CONNECTIONS

Three new houses (below) have been built along a highway in Alaska. Each house needs an electricity supply and a water supply; however the permafrost means nothing can be buried underground, and no supply must ever cross a driveway. Also, a new safety law states that no electricity supply may cross a water pipeline.

Can the houses be connected up?

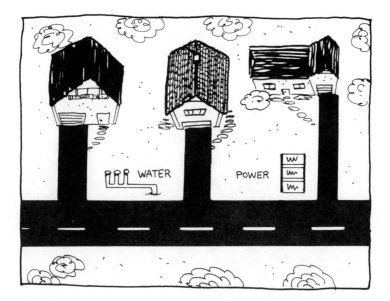

CUBE OF CHEESE

Honoria was hosting a party—entertaining some friends. She had planned a specially elegant dinner, and wanted a cube of cheese as part of an appetizer display.

Looking in the refrigerator, she found she did have some cheese, but it was in the form of a complete sphere; in other words, a ball of cheese. Well, she would simply have to cut a cube of cheese from the cheese ball.

Honoria can't resist a puzzle so she spent most of the time as she prepared dinner wondering how to cut the sphere of cheese into a cube quickly; that is, using the fewest number of cuts.

What is the smallest number of cuts you have to make to cut a cube from a sphere?

CRATE EXPECTATIONS

You have six bottles of pop for a party, and you want to arrange them in an attractive pattern in the crate. Four will make a square...

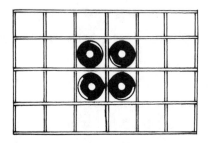

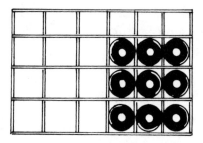

and nine will make a square. But six is a trickier number. How about an even number of bottles in each line?

Can you arrange them so that, in every row and in every column, the number of bottles is even (0, 2, 4, or 6)?

THE PIZZA AND THE SWORD

The room is full of hungry people. You have just had delivered a monster pizza, which covers most of the table. It's too hot to touch, but you need to cut it up quickly so that everyone can start eating.

What is the maximum number of pieces you can make with three straight cuts across? You may not move the pieces until you have finished cutting; so you can't pile them on top of one another!

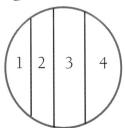

You could make the three cuts side by side, which would give you one extra piece for each cut; so you would get four pieces altogether.

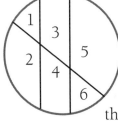

Or, you could make two cuts side by side, and then the third across both of them. That would give you six pieces. But could you make more than six?

Hint Nobody said the pieces all have to be the same size; indeed it would be better if they were all different sizes!

PENCIL SQUARES

Lay 15 pencils (or straws, toothpicks or what you have) out on the table to make five equal squares like this:

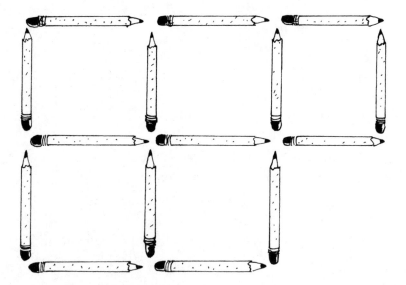

Now take away just three of the pencils, and leave only three squares.

PENCIL TRIANGLES

Here's a really tough puzzle that you can use to stump your friends, after you have figured it out. If you are able to solve it without peeking at the solution, you are doing better than a whole lot of brilliant people.

This time, take 6 pencils (or straws or toothpicks) and arrange them so that they form four equal triangles.

THE ROLLING QUARTER

Imagine a quarter laid on the table and fixed there, perhaps with a dab of glue. Now lay another quarter against it, and roll the second quarter all the way around the first one, without any slipping at the edges, until it gets back to where it started.

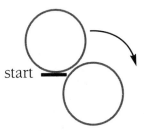

In making one complete circuit, how many times does the second quarter rotate?

SLIDING QUARTERS

Here's a puzzle that looks simple, but is really quite tricky. Even when you have seen the answer you sometimes can't remember it. Maybe you are smart enough to solve it on your own, but if you go on to baffle your friends, make sure you can remember the solution when you need it!

Lay six quarters on the table touching in two rows of three, like this:

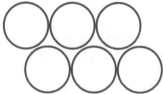

In each move, slide one quarter, without moving any others, until it just touches two others. In only three moves, can you get them into a circle like this?

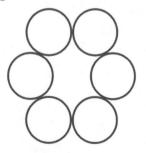

FIND THE GOLD

Lucy Sly, a brilliant detective, has tracked some pirates to their island base. In their secret cave, she finds the pirate chief with three chests of treasure. One chest contains pieces of iron, one chest pieces of gold, and the third has a mixture.

In return for a chance to escape, the pirate chief offers Lucy one chest to take away with her. All three chests are labeled—IRON, GOLD, and MIXTURE. But, he warns her, all the labels are on the wrong chests.

"Then I can't tell which is which," she replies.

"I will take one object out of any one of these chests, and show it to you—although you may not look inside."

Which chest would you choose to see an object from? And how would you be sure you got the chest of gold?

FRISKY FROGS

Across a stream runs a row of seven stepping stones.

On one side of the stream, sitting on the first three stones, are three girl frogs, Fergie, Francine, and Freda, and they want to get across to the other side.

There's an empty stone in the middle.

On the other side are three boy frogs, waiting to come across the other way—Fred, Frank, and Frambo.

Only one frog moves at a time. Any frog may hop to the next stone if it is empty, or may hop over one frog of the opposite sex onto an empty stone.

Can you get all the frogs across the river?

LEAPING LIZARDS

Across a stream runs a row of eight stepping stones.

On one side of the stream, on the first five stones, sit five girl lizards—Liza, Lizzie, Lottie, Lola, and Liz— and they want to get across to the other side.

There's one empty stone in the middle.

On the other side are three boy lizards, waiting to come across the other way—Lonnie, Leo, and Len.

Only one lizard moves at a time. Any lizard may hop to the next stone if it is empty, or may hop over one lizard of the opposite sex onto an empty stone.

Can you get all the lizards across the river, and what's the smallest number of leaps?

PICNIC MYSTERY

Allie takes fruit, cake, and cookies for her picnic. She has three boxes for them. One is labeled FRUIT. One is labeled COOKIES. One is labeled CAKE. But she knows her Mom likes to fool her and has put every single thing in the wrong box. The only other thing she knows for sure is that the fruit is not in the CAKE box.

Where is the cake?

WIENER TRIANGLES

In the link-wiener factory in Sausageville, the wieners are made in long strings, with a link of skin holding each sausage to the next one. So, although the wieners are firm, you can bend the string of wieners around into many shapes. For example, you can easily bend a string of 3 wieners into a triangle.

Suppose you had a string of 9 wieners. Without breaking the string, how many triangles can you make?

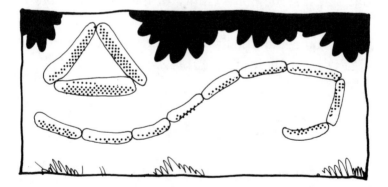

TENNIS TOURNAMENT

You successfully arranged a "knock-out" tennis tournament, in which the winners of the first round meet in the second round, and so on. The little tournament had only four players, so arranging it was easy.

In the first round, Eenie played Meanie, and Eenie won. Miney played Mo, and Mo went through to the second round. In the second round—the final—Mo beat Eenie, and won the tournament.

The 3-game match card looked like this:

The match was so well organized, you've been asked to arrange another knock-out tennis tournament. This time 27 players enter. How many matches will have to be played to find the winner?

MAGIC HEXAGON

Here is a section of a honeycomb—seven hexagons in a group.

Can you write the numbers 1 through 7, one in each hexagon, so that all three lines across the middle add up to a total of 12?

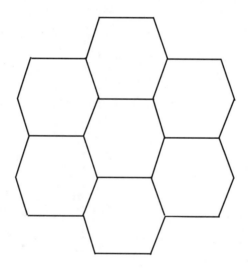

THREE SISTERS

Three sisters, Ady, Beadie, and Cedie, went out into the wide world and found jobs; one of them became an architect, one a builder, and the third a cook. Then they married Mr. Able, Dr. Baker, and Charlie. None of the first letters in their first and last names or occupations match up—so Mr. Able is not married to Ady, and she is not the architect. If Charlie's wife isn't a builder, who married the doctor?

THE POWER OF SEVEN

Far back in history, a lonely fort was being desperately defended against thousands of attackers.

The attacks came regularly at noon every day, and the defending commander knew he had to survive only three more days, for then would come the end of the attackers' calendar, and they would all go home to celebrate, giving time for his reinforcements to arrive.

He also knew that the attackers held an unshakable belief in the power of the number 7. So he always placed 7 defenders on each wall of the fort. With three attacks to come, and only 24 defenders, he places 5 along each wall, and 1 in each corner tower.

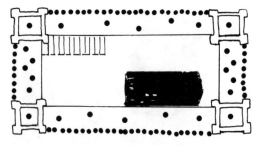

The attackers charge in from the north, and see 7 defenders along that wall. Firing a volley of arrows, they wheel round and retreat, chanting "Neves! Neves!" meaning seven in their language. They charge from the west and again see 7 defenders facing them. Firing a volley of arrows they retreat again. "Neves! Neves!"

From the south then the east, again they charge. Each time they are met by exactly 7 defenders. Each time they turn and flee, chanting "Neves! Neves!" And the attack is over for the day.

The commander mops his worried brow as the bugler blows the bugle to signal "Well done and all clear!" Then he learns the arrows have killed 4 of his men.

How can he rearrange the remaining 20 so that by noon of the next day there will still be 7 defenders on each side?

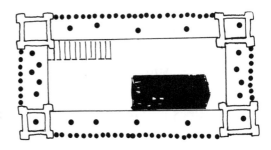

BUNDLES OF TUBES

William Posters set up a company to make cardboard tubes and sell them for the protection of large pictures or posters sent through the mail. He advertised:

KEEP YOUR POSTERS SAFE WITH BILL POSTERS' TUBES!

He makes some tubes 2 inches in diameter and some 3 inches in diameter, for extra big posters. He sells the bigger tubes in bundles of 19, and the smaller tubes in bundles of 37.

Most people sell things in tens, or dozens, or even packets of 25. Why do you think he chose 19 and 37?

HOUSE COLORS

George and Greg Green both live with their families in big houses on Route 1, just outside town, and their sister Bernice, married to Bert Blue, lives in the third house on the same road.

One day, they all secretly decided to paint their houses the same color as their names, and were glad to find out afterwards that no next-door houses were the same color.

Who lives in the middle house of the three?

THREE J'S

Joan and Jane are sisters. Jean is Joan's daughter, and 12 years younger than her aunt.

Joan is twice as old as Jean.

Four years ago, Joan was the same age as Jane is now, and Jane was twice as old as her niece.

How old is Jean?

CUTTING THE HORSESHOE

Here's a picture of a horseshoe.

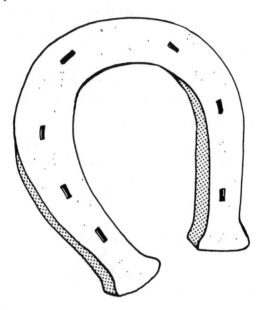

Your challenge is to cut it into seven pieces, each containing a nail hole, with just two straight cuts. After the first cut, you can put the pieces on top of one another, but both cuts have to be straight.

Can you make seven "holey" pieces?

NO BURGLARS!

Worried by the number of burglaries in your town, you have just installed Fantastico High-Security Locks on all the doors in your house. They are so special that you actually have to walk through a doorway and lock the door behind you, and then it cannot be opened by anyone else.

Here is a plan of your house:

A = bedroom
B = hall
C = dining room
D = bathroom
E = living room
F = kitchen
G = den

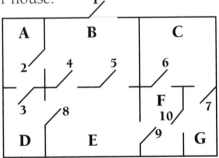

You decide to go out to the movies. You need to go through and lock each door, ending with the front door.

In which room would you start? And in which order would you shut the doors behind you to make sure you went through and locked every one?

PUZZLE OF THE SPHINX

Here are four little sphinxes, small versions of the big one found in the Egyption desert.

How can you rearrange these four sphinx shapes to make one big sphinx?

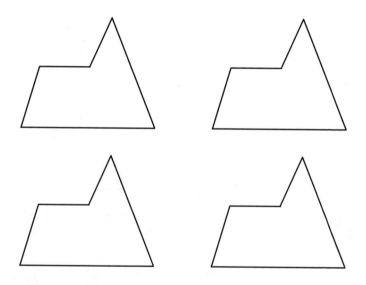

Hint It's really just a small jigsaw puzzle, except that one of the "pieces" fits in *backwards*.

PERFORATION!

You have 12 postage stamps that have a picture of your favorite flower on each.

You want to put them in your stamp book, but it's made for 3 rows of 4 stamps like this, not 4 rows of 3.

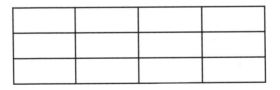

How can you tear the sheet of stamps, along the perforations, into only two pieces so that they will fit together and fill your page better?

WILD GEESE

Aunt Rody has nine wild geese in a big square pen. The trouble is, they are so wild they keep fighting; so she decides to separate them all.

Where can she build two more square pens so that all the geese are separated?

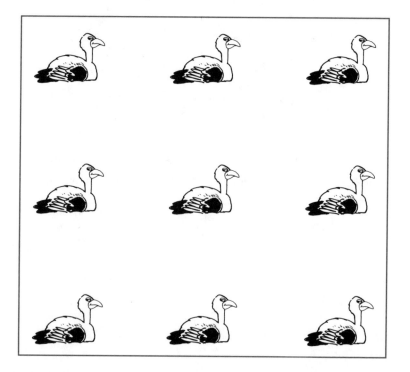

BEEFY BISON

In 1976, in honor of 200 years of American Independence (USA bicentennial), Aunt Rhody started a bison ranch, keeping 16 bison in a big field. She's kept the bison fenced-in in groups of 2, 3, 3, and 8. Now she wants to change it to groups of 4, 6, and 6.

How can she do this by moving only two fences?

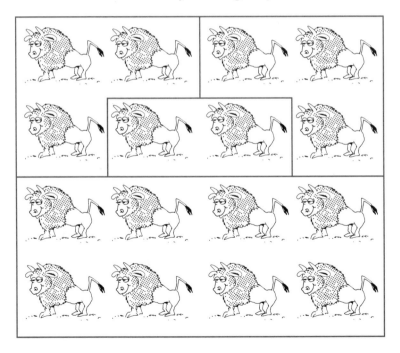

COLORED BALLS #1

You have five red balls,

five yellow balls,

and five blue balls.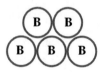

How can you arrange them in this triangular frame so that no two balls of the same color are next to one another?

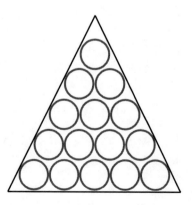

LOGICAL POP

You have three identical cans. One is labeled POP, one is labeled MILK SHAKE, and one is labeled POTATO CHIPS.

However, you know your mischievous sister has, as a joke, changed all the labels, so that every label is on the wrong can.

You want to open the pop, but you are allowed to open only one can; so you have to get it right.

To get a clue, you may shake one can first. Which one would you shake, and how would you choose which can to open?

HOW MANY DUCKS?

Little Francine saw some ducks going through a gap in the hedge and out into the field. She had never seen any ducks before; so she was excited by the little procession.

When she told her aunt about them later, her aunt asked how many ducks she had seen.

"Well," said Francine, "I'm not much good at counting, but there was a duck in front of a duck and a duck behind a duck and a duck in the middle."

What is the smallest number of ducks she could have seen?

POOL OF GLUE

When the teacher Miss Take comes into her second grade classroom, she is about to sit down when she sees a pool of glue on her chair.

There are only three girls in the room, Pansy Potter, Peony Plummer, and Petal Prancer, and there is no way anyone else could have left the room. So one of the three must have put the glue there.

Miss Take immediately questions the three girls:

Pansy Potter says, "It was Peony that poured the glue on your chair!"
Peony Plummer says, "No; it was Petal!"
Petal Prancer says, "I didn't do it!"

Two of the girls are telling the truth, but one is lying. Who is the guilty one?

UPENDING THE CUPS

Make yourself a row of seven plastic cups or mugs or paper water cups, all turned upside-down on the table.

The challenge is to turn them the right way up, but always turning over three at a time. So after your first turn they might look like this:

...or like this:

How can you turn them all the right way up, in just three goes?

PUZZLING SAND

Builder Bill needs exactly 11 pounds of sand to mix with cement, but when he goes to the sand supplier he is presented with a puzzle. The supplier has plenty of sand, and two big boxes on a balance, but he has only two weights: a 4-pound weight and a 5-pound weight.

He tells Bill, "If you can weigh out exactly 11 pounds into one of the boxes, without taking any sand out of either, you can have your sand for free!"

Bill puzzled and puzzled, and started pouring sand. Suddenly he saw how to do it.

What did he do?

SECRET NUMBER CODES

To send a secret message to a friend, send the message in code so that no one else can read what it says. Of course, your friend needs to know how to decode the message, so only the two of you will understand.

This simple code changes each letter to a number:

A	B	C	D	E	F	G	H	I	J	K	L	M
1	2	3	4	5	6	7	8	9	10	11	12	13

N	O	P	Q	R	S	T	U	V	W	X	Y	Z
14	15	16	17	18	19	20	21	22	23	24	25	26

To send the message MEET ME AT SIX you write down their numbers instead of the letters:

13 5 5 20   13 5   1 20   19 9 24

But clever people might be able to guess this code, so you might want to make yours a little more complicated. See if you can work out what this message means:

14 6 6 21   14 6   2 21   20 6 23 6 15

SWEET SPOT

This is the toughest puzzle in the book. If you can solve it without peeking, you are a genius.

Windy, Wendy, and Woody sat in a triangle, facing one another. Their teacher said the brightest could have a candy bar. "I have here three white spots, and two black ones. I shall put one spot on each of your foreheads, so that you can see the others' spots, but not your own. The first to tell me what color you are, and how you know, wins the candy."

Then he stuck a white spot on each of their foreheads, making sure none of them could see any spots except those on the other two heads.

After a minute, Wendy stood up. "I'm a white spot!"

"Sure?"

"Sure I'm sure."

How did Wendy know?

TRICKY ARITHMETIC
PUZZLES

WAITING IN LINE

At the local sandwich shop, every customer who enters is given a number. On one particularly busy lunch hour, customers 17 through 31 were waiting to be called.

If you counted up all the waiting customers, how many would there be?

WHO IS FASTER?

Hector can run from the train station to his parents' house in eight minutes. His younger brother Darius can run the same distance eight times in one hour. (Not that he'd need to!) Who is faster?

THE AVERAGE STUDENT

Melissa got a poor grade on her very first homework assignment at her new school—only one star out of a possible five stars! She was determined to do better. How many five-star ratings must she receive before she has an *AVERAGE* rating of four stars?

Hint Knowing that the average of the ratings must be four, you start out with a three-point difference between the one-star rating (given to Melissa on her first assignment) and the desired four-star average. Well, how many stars can you make up at a time?!

BIG DIFFERENCE

Your challenge is to place the digits 2, 4, 6, and 7 into the boxes so that the difference between the two two-digit numbers is as big as possible.

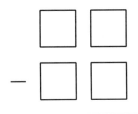

NOT SUCH A BIG DIFFERENCE

What if you wanted to make the difference as *SMALL* as possible?

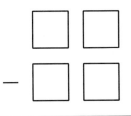

(Big Difference) Hint To find the biggest difference, try creating the biggest possible number.

(Not Such a Big Difference) Hint Find two numbers that are close together.

SHORT DIVISION

See if you can perform the following division problem—without writing below the line!

$$7 \overline{)\, 497{,}637{,}357}$$

THE MISSING SIX

Place the six numbers below into the empty circles so that both sentences are true. Use each number once and only once.

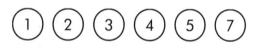

$$\bigcirc + \bigcirc = \bigcirc$$

$$\bigcirc - \bigcirc = \bigcirc$$

(Short Division) Hint: The big number can be broken into many pieces, each of which is divisible by 7.

(The Missing Six) Hint: More trial and error. If the "7" in the puzzle was replaced by a "6," no answer would be possible.

TRICK OR TREAT

Halloween night was almost over, and fewer than 20 candies remained at the Greensleeve household. When the doorbell rang, Mr. Greensleeve figured it was the final group of trick-or-treaters for the night, so he figured he'd give away the rest of his candy.

At the door were two kids, one dressed as a ghost and the other as a lion. Mr. Greensleeve wanted to give them the same number of candies, but he noticed that when he split the candies up, there was one left over.

At that point he noticed that a witch was hiding behind the lion. Now there were three trick-or-treaters. He tried dividing the candies equally among the three, but, again, one candy was left over.

Finally, Dracula jumped out from behind the ghost. Mr. Greensleeve tried dividing the candies among the *four* trick-or-treaters, but again there was one left over.

How many candies did Mr. Greensleeve have left when the doorbell rang?

Hint Remember, Mr. Greensleeve has fewer than 20 candies remaining, and many possibilities can be ruled out immediately. Try listing the numbers from 1 to 20 and crossing them out as you go along.

DONUT TRY THIS AT HOME

Suppose a low-calorie donut has 95 percent fewer calories than a regular donut. How many low-calorie donuts would you need to eat to take in as many calories as you'd get from a regular donut?

Hint If a regular donut has, say, 100 calories, how many does a low-calorie donut have?

THE LONG WAY AROUND

If the height of the diagram on the next page is 8 units, and the length is 15 units, how far is it around the entire diagram?

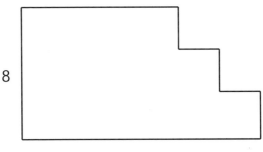

8

15

problem. We guarantee it!
Remember, you *do* have enough information to solve the
Hint Do the "steps" in the figure really change anything?

STARTING TO WAFFLE

A portable waffle machine makes 120 waffles per minute.
A stationary waffle machine makes 3 waffles per second.
How many portable machines would you need if you
wanted to equal the output of 4 stationary machines?

PLOP!

Hint: Translate the rate of the portable machine into waffles per
second. That way you can compare the two rates directly.

A VERY GOOD YEAR

The year 1978 has an unusual property: When you add the 19 to the 78, you get 97—the middle two digits of the year!

What will be the next year to have this same property?

Hint: The year could not be in the 2000s or the 2100s, because the middle number would start off less than the first two digits. So start with the year 2200 and work from there. You need to do a little trial and error—but not too much!

TWO WORKERS ARE BETTER THAN ONE

If one worker can complete a job in 6 days and a second worker takes 12 days to complete the same job, how long will it take them working together?

Hint One way to figure out the problem is to find out what portion of the job each worker accomplishes in one day. But if you don't want to work with fractions, just ask what the two workers would accomplish in 12 days—working together, of course.

AN ODD GAME OF BINGO

Imagine playing a game of bingo using the card on page 57, on which all the numbers are odd!

The idea behind this particular game is that you must get a bingo—either across, up and down, or diagonally—that adds up to precisely 100. This can only be done in one way. Do you see how?

23	11	25	15	41
1	37	31	5	17
9	21	FREE	27	47
43	35	33	29	7
19	45	3	39	13

Hint Some of the rows are just too big to add to 100. But there's another clue: Is 100 odd or even? Is the sum of five odd numbers odd or even? You don't have to do much actual addition to solve this problem, because you can rule out many of the answers before you even begin!

THE PRICE OF FUN

A Frisbee and a softball together cost $6.20. The Frisbee costs $1.20 more than the softball. How much does the Frisbee cost?

Hint You don't need algebra to solve this puzzle, though it would help. A little trial and error should see you through, but you'd better make sure that the difference between the cost of the two items is $1.20.

FARE WARS

Suppose a taxicab in Megalopolis charges 75 cents for the first quarter-mile and 15 cents for each additional quarter-mile. In Cloud City, a taxi charges $1.00 for the first quarter-mile and 10 cents for each additional quarter-mile.

What distance would produce the same fare for the two taxicabs?

Hint What is the initial cost difference between the two cabs? How does it change every quarter-mile?

THE POWERS OF FOUR

Bert and Ernie take turns multiplying numbers. First Bert chooses the number 4. Ernie multiplies it by 4 to get 16. Bert multiplies that by 4 to get 64. Ernie multiplies that by 4 to get 256.

After going back and forth several times, one of them comes up with the number 1,048,576. Who came up with that number, Bert or Ernie?

Don't worry—the problem is easier than it looks at first glance. You don't have to multiply the whole thing out to figure out the correct answer!

Hint If you kept multiplying by 4, that would lead you to the right answer, but an easier approach is to look for patterns.

HIGH-SPEED COPYING

If 4 copiers can process 400 sheets of paper in 4 hours, how long does it take 8 copiers to process 800 sheets?

Hint: Questions like this one have been around for a lot longer than there have been copiers! The best approach is to look at the number of copies an individual can make, and go on from there.

DIVIDE AND CONQUER

Fill in the boxes at right to make the division problem work out.

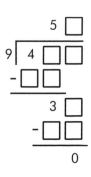

AGENT 86

Fill in the missing squares in such a way that the rows, columns, and the two diagonals all add up to the same number.

32	19		8
10	25		
9			
35	16		11

(Agent 86) Hint If you add up the numbers in the first column, you will find out the sum for every row, column, or diagonal. Then go on to those rows or columns containing three out of the four possible numbers, and you'll be able to figure out the fourth. Pretty soon you'll be all done!

(Divide and Conquer) Hint Start by multiplying the 5 and the 9 to get the second row of the division. That should get you rolling.

COMIC RELIEF

While traveling in Russia, I bought six comic books for a total of seventeen rubles. Some of the comics cost one ruble, others cost two rubles, while the most expensive ones sold for ten rubles apiece.

How many of each type did I buy?

Hint How many ten-ruble comic books can there be?

A PANE IN THE NECK

The window in Harvey's living room has gotten very dirty. He asks a window washer how long the job will take, and the window washer says that it takes him 30 seconds to clean each 6 x 10 region. Harvey thinks that's a strange answer, until he realizes that 6 x 10 is the size of an individual pane. Well, how long will the entire job take?

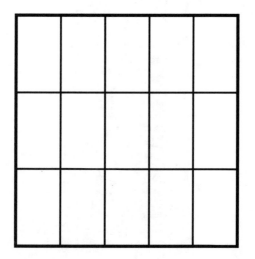

Hint Remember that when the window washer has finished the job, Harvey should be able to see out the window perfectly.

PUTTING YOUR TWO CENTS IN

Many years ago, when things cost less than they do today, two brothers—Aaron and Bobby—went to the corner drugstore to purchase a pad of paper. Unfortunately, neither brother had much money. Aaron realized that he was two cents short, while Bobby was twenty four cents short. When they put their money together, they found that they still didn't have enough to purchase the pad! How much does the pad cost?

SURF'S UP

At a surf shop in Malibu, California, a used blue surfboard is on sale for 100 dollars. According to the salesperson, the new price represents a 20% discount from the original price. What did it sell for originally?

Hint A common guess is $120, but that's not right.

APPLE PICKING

Seventh Heaven Orchards decides to hold a special sale at the end of the season, hoping that people will come and buy the apples that have already fallen from the

trees! They decide on an unusual system for pricing the apples. The bags they give out hold just seven apples each. The orchard then charges its customers five cents for every bag of seven apples, and 15 cents for every apple left over!

According to this system, which costs the most: 10 apples, 30 apples, or 50 apples?

Hint There is nothing tricky about the calculations here, but the answer may be a surprise.

PLAYING THE TRIANGLE

The triangle in the diagram has the lengths of two sides labeled. The reason the third side isn't labeled is that the labeler couldn't remember whether that side was 5 units long, 11 units long, or 21 units long. Can you figure out which it is? (Sorry, but the diagram is not drawn to scale!)

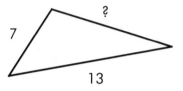

IT ALL ADDS UP

The sum of the digits of a certain three-digit number is 12. If the hundreds digit is three times the tens digit, and the tens digit is one-half the ones digit, what is the number?

(**Playing the Triangle**) **Hint** It is not possible to take just any three numbers and form a triangle with those numbers as the lengths of the sides. Remember, the shortest path between two points is a straight line.

(**It All Adds Up**) **Hint** The most a single digit can be is nine, so you don't have that many choices.

GENERATION GAP

Grandpa Jones has four grandchildren. Each grandchild is precisely one year older than the next oldest one. One year Jones noticed that if you added the ages of his four grandchildren, you would get his age. How old is Grandpa Jones?

A) 76
B) 78
C) 80

TALKING ABOUT MY GENERATION!

Hint Trial and error may work out here. You might also save some time if you notice that one of the three ages has a property that the other two do not have.

THE FRENCH CONNECTION

Jason and Sandy took five tests during their first year in French class. Jason's scores were 72, 85, 76, 81, and 91. Sandy's scores were 94, 79, 84, 75, and 88. How much higher was Sandy's average score than Jason's average score?

Hint You can figure out the average grade for each student by adding up the individual test scores and dividing by five. But if you look closely at the test scores, you may find a shortcut.

THE LONG ROAD

If you perform all the operations that are indicated, and end up with the number 97 in the circle, what number did you start with?

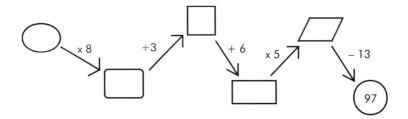

Hint This problem has to be done backwards. Work from right to left, and do the opposite of what you're told to do!

IF THE SHOE FITS

A town has 20,000 people living in it. Five percent of them are one-legged, and half of the rest go barefoot. How many shoes are worn by the people in the town?

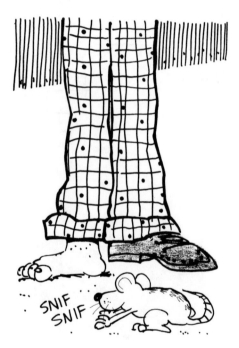

SNIF
SNIF

Hint Read the puzzle carefully. On the other hand, it might interest you to know that the number five—as in five percent—doesn't really have much to do with the solution.

WE CAN WORK IT OUT

The dot-filled diagram is from an exercise bicycle at the health club. The numbers on the left stand for the degree of difficulty of the exercise. The higher the number, the greater the resistance offered by the bike, which increases the workout. The columns represent time: Each column stands for 10 seconds at the specified level.

But we don't have to worry about all that, because our task is a mental challenge, not a physical one. How many dots are there in all?

One last piece of advice: Don't count the dots one by one, or you'll go dizzy. There's a better way!

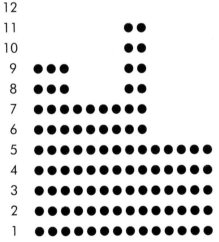

Hint The problem is best tackled by separating the dots into rectangles. Just figure out the number of dots in each rectangle, then add them up.

DON'T SNEEZE, PLEASE

If the doctor says to take an allergy pill every three hours, how much time will go by between the first pill and the fourth pill?

...THIS PILL IS NOTHING TO SNEEZE AT!

STORE 24

Using six 1's and three plus signs, can you form an expression that equals 24?

(**Don't Sneeze, Please**) **Hint** Another trick question. Read it carefully, and put yourself in the position of the person who is taking the pills—even if you don't have allergies!

(**Store 24**) **Hint** All you have to do is put the 1's together in the right way.

THICK AS A BRICK

If the diagram shows one face of a chimney, how many bricks are required to build the entire chimney? Remember, no bricks are cut in half.

ON ALL FOURS

Using just basic addition, subtraction, multiplication, and division, can you form each of the numbers from 1 through 10 using precisely four 4's?

To give you an idea of how this works, we'll start you off:

$$1 = (4+4)/(4+4)$$
$$2 = (4x4)/(4+4).$$

The rest is up to you!

(Thick as a Brick) Hint How many bricks are required to build a single row?

(On All Fours) Hint It might help to know that you can create 0 with two 4's $(4 - 4)$ and 1 with two 4's $(4/4)$. These are useful building blocks in making the numbers 1 through 10.

HOUSE OF CARDS

In the diagram below, nine playing cards are set up to form a rectangle. Assuming that the area of the rectangle is 180 square inches, what is its perimeter? (The perimeter is the distance around the entire rectangle.)

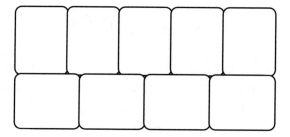

Hint Figure out the dimensions of each individual card.

ONCE IN A CENTURY

In Eleventown, the citizens hold a big parade on January 1st of every year that is divisible by the number 11.

Well, a funny thing happened during the 1900s. As you recall, the nineteen hundreds were divided into ten decades, as follows:

The aughts:	1900–1909	The fifties:	1950–1959
The teens:	1910–1919	The sixties:	1960–1969
The twenties:	1920–1929	The seventies:	1970–1979
The thirties:	1930–1939	The eighties:	1980–1989
The forties:	1940–1949	The nineties:	1990–1999

In one and only one of these decades, there is no number divisible by 11. In which decade was there no parade in Eleventown?

Hint One of the toughest problems in this book. The key fact is that if a set of ten consecutive numbers contains no multiple of 11, then the very next number must be a multiple of 11. So if a decade—which ends in a year ending in 9—does not contain a multiple of 11, then one of the numbers of the form 1910, 1920, 1930, etc. is divisible by 11. The answer is the decade that comes *before* this number!

THE CONVERSION MACHINE

If you give the conversion machine a number, it will put the number through three separate steps. First of all, the machine will divide the number by 5. Then it will multiply the new number by 9. Finally, the machine will subtract 32 from the result.

One of the following numbers *remains the same* after it has been put through all three stages of the conversion machine. Which one is it?

A) 10

B) 20

C) 30

D) 40

Hint This one is pretty simple. Just follow the same rules as the machine, and you'll find the magic number.

THE EASY WAY OUT

What is (138 x 109) + (164 x 138) + (138 x 227)? Can you do it without multiplying everything out?

SEE YOU LATER, CALCULATOR!

Which is bigger, 18 percent of 87, or 87 percent of 18? And don't multiply this out!

(The Easy Way Out) Hint Don't perform the indicated multiplications. Note that 138 is repeated in all three expressions. Even better, the other numbers add up to a nice round number.

(See You Later, Calculator!) Hint Remember, you don't need to make any calculations to solve this one—or have you forgotten the title already? Common sense is the winner here.

KANGAROO NUMBERS

A kangaroo number is a number that shows one of its factors. For example, any number with a zero at the end is a kangaroo number— 560 has 56 as a factor. (5 also divides evenly into 560, but to be a kangaroo number, the factor must be more than one digit long.) The digits also have to be in order. (In 560, 56 is a factor, but 65 is not.)

Now that you know how they work, which of the following numbers are kangaroo numbers?

    A) 125
    B) 664
    C) 729
    D) 912

BLIND DATE

Choose a weekday between October 9 and October 20 in the calendar below. Add to it all the numbers in the 3 x 3 square that surround it. Now divide this total by 9. What is your answer?

OCTOBER 2000

S	M	T	W	T	F	S
1	2	3	4	5	6	7
8	9	10	11	12	13	14
15	16	17	18	19	20	21
22	23	24	25	26	27	28
29	30	31				

Hint The hint is that you're looking right at the answer!

A GAME OF CHICKEN

Chicken McNuggets come in packages of 6, 9, and 20. Suppose you wanted to purchase 99 McNuggets for you and your friends. Assuming you wanted to buy as few individual packages as possible, how many of each size would you order?

WOULD YOU LIKE *FRIES* WITH THAT?

REEL LIFE STORY

A group of seven adults went to the movies. The total cost of the movie tickets was $30.

This doesn't seem possible, does it? After all, 30 is not evenly divisible by 7. Ah, but there's a hitch. The reason that $30 *was* the total cost was that some members of the group were senior citizens, so they got to see the movie at half price.

How many of the group were senior citizens, and how much did the tickets cost?

Hint Trial and error will win the day. Note that the price of a senior ticket must divide evenly into 30.

JACK IN THE BOX

Of six cards chosen from a full deck of playing cards, two are jacks. Suppose you placed all six cards in a box and selected two at random. Which is more likely—that you will select at least one jack or that you will select no jacks at all?

I DON'T KNOW JACK!!

Hint Count out all the possibilities and see how many involve no jacks.

THE RIGHT STUFF

Ninety people applied for a job as a salesperson for a book publishing company. Ten of the applicants had never worked in sales or in the publishing business. Sixty-five had worked in sales at some point, and fifty-eight had some background in publishing.

How many of the applicants had experience in *both* sales and publishing?

Hint If you add up all the numbers, you'll get something way too big. But you're on the right track as long as you subtract the right number from your total.

THE TWELVE DAYS OF CHRISTMAS

The song "The Twelve Days of Christmas" includes some well-known presents:

A partridge in a pear tree
Two turtle doves
Three French hens
Four calling birds
Five golden rings
Six geese a-laying
Seven swans a-swimming
Eight maids a-milking
Nine drummers drumming
Ten pipers piping
Eleven dancers dancing
Twelve lords a-leaping

Throughout the entire song, including all twelve "verses," which present shows up most often? (For example, "two turtle doves" counts as *two* presents every time that phrase is sung.)

OH, BROTHER!

Jeff was watching his older brother Matt do his math homework. Matt said that the assignment was about factorials, a subject much too complicated for Jeff to understand.

"What's the exclamation point?" Jeff asked, looking at the strange expression 8! in the middle of his brother's notes.

"It's a factorial symbol," Matt said.

"Well, what's a factorial?" Jeff asked.

Matt said, "A factorial is when you take all the whole numbers less than or equal to a particular number and multiply them all together. So 10! = 10 x 9 x 8 x 7 x 6 x 5 x 4 x 3 x 2 x 1. Now do you believe me when I say these things are hard?"

"I guess so," Jeff said. "But what's the problem you're working on?"

"I have to figure out what 8! divided by 6! is," Matt said.

Two seconds later, Jeff said, "I see the answer."

How did Jeff figure out what 8!/6! was without multiplying the whole thing out?

Hint Don't worry about the exclamation point. You don't have to multiply out either 8! or 7!, but you *do* need to see that "cancellation" makes the problem easier.

NUMBERS ON THE HOUSE

Suppose the town planning commission decides to buy brand-new house numbers for all of the residents of Sleepy Hollow Road. There are 50 houses on the road, numbered 1–50. How many of each number will they need?

Hint Count them up by considering the tens place and the ones place individually. Then put the totals together.

SQUARE FEET

A group of soldiers was marching in a square formation when 32 of them were called off for a training mission. The remaining soldiers regrouped and continued their marching, this time forming a smaller square. They continued to march until eight of them had to leave to run an obstacle course.

How many soldiers were there originally?

Hint The question is, what number is a perfect square and stays a perfect square when you subtract 32 from it? Don't worry, the number of soldiers is less than 100, so the number of soldiers on either side of the square is a single-digit number. But remember that the second square must have more than eight men in it.

INCOMPLETE SENTENCES

Place the appropriate sign—addition, subtraction, multiplication, or division—between the numbers 6, 3, and 2 to make the following number sentences true.

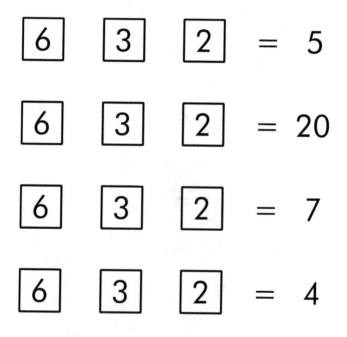

$$6 \quad 3 \quad 2 \quad = \quad 5$$

$$6 \quad 3 \quad 2 \quad = \quad 20$$

$$6 \quad 3 \quad 2 \quad = \quad 7$$

$$6 \quad 3 \quad 2 \quad = \quad 4$$

Hint Remember that you perform the various operations (addition, subtraction, multiplication, division) from left to right.

HE WAS FRAMED!

Jennifer bought a picture frame for a 4" x 6" picture of her boyfriend. The outside of the frame measures 5" x 7". If the picture fits inside perfectly, how wide is the frame?

DOUBLE TROUBLE

It is possible to place the numbers 1 through 9 in the nine boxes below so that both of the multiplications in the sequence are correct. The numbers 3, 7, 8, and 9 have been placed for you. Can you figure out where the other five numbers go?

$$\boxed{}\,\boxed{8}\,\times\,\boxed{3}\,=\,\boxed{}\,\boxed{7}\,\boxed{}\,=\,\boxed{}\,\boxed{9}\,\times\,\boxed{}$$

(Double Trouble) Hint You can figure out the ones digit of the three-digit number from the information you have already. Then try and figure out the missing number on the far left.

(He Was Framed!) Hint This is a trick question. The answer is *not* one inch.

MISERY LOVES COMPANY

Two investors—we'll call them Smith and Jones—made some unfortunate decisions in the stock market: Smith lost 60% of his money and Jones lost 85%. Jones was so discouraged he took his money out and put it into a savings bank. Smith, on the other hand, made some additional investments in an effort to get his money back. But he wasn't any luckier the second time around—he lost *ANOTHER* 60%!

Well, neither of them made a very strong showing, that much is certain. But who did worse, Smith or Jones?

Hint Suppose they each started out with one thousand dollars. After the first losses, Smith had $400 and Jones had $150. Now you have to work out how much Smith had left after his second 60% loss. (We are not including any interest that Jones might have earned from his savings account.)

STRANGE BUT TRUE

Melanie was given three positive numbers and told to add them up. Jessica was given the same three numbers and told to multiply them all together. Surprise, surprise: Melanie and Jessica got the same answer!

What numbers were they given?

Hint Don't look too far. As a general rule, the bigger the numbers you choose, the greater the difference will be between their sum and their product. And if that's true for two numbers, it's certainly true for three!

SAY THE MAGIC WORDS

Three favorite words of magicians are ABRACADABRA, PRESTO, and SHAZAM! If each letter is given a value from its position in the alphabet (A = 1, B = 2, and so on), and you add up the values for each word, which would have the highest value?

Hint Just because a word is long that doesn't mean its "value" is high. Check out all the As in ABRACADABRA!

A FAMOUS TRIANGLE

The diagram shows the first six rows of a famous mathematical construction called Pascal's Triangle. The way the triangle works is that 1's are placed on the outside edges, and each number on the inside is the sum of the two numbers above it. For example, the 6 in the middle of the fifth row is the sum of the two 3's from the fourth row.

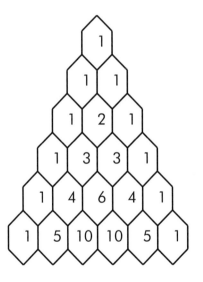

Okay, now that you know what Pascal's Triangle is, what is the sum of all the elements of the unseen *seventh* row?

Note: You don't have to figure out the numbers in the seventh row in order to figure out its sum!

Hint See if you can find a pattern in the sums of the first six rows.

FOLLOW THE DIRECTIONS

There are several different ways of putting the numbers 1 through 5 into the circles below so that both directions—North-South and East-West—add up to the same number. But your question is a different one: Whatever way you happen to choose, the middle number will be the same. What is that number?

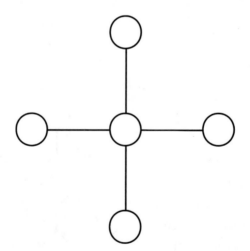

Hint You can solve the puzzle by trial and error, and the middle number of any solution is the middle number of *every* solution! But there's also a common sense approach that might give you the answer even without placing numbers in all five positions.

LETTER LOGIC

In the addition below each letter stands for a number. Different letters must stand for different numbers, and if the same letter is repeated, it must stand for the same number each time. To give you a head start, one of the numbers has been revealed to be a 5.

$$\begin{array}{r} \text{END} \\ + \ \text{5G} \\ \hline \text{GAME} \end{array}$$

1) What must the "G" stand for?
2) What must the "E" stand for?
3) Can you solve the entire puzzle?

Hint To figure out G, remember that "END" and "5G" are fairly small relative to "GAME." Once you have G, you can figure out A and E using the same idea. And once you have G and E you automatically have D, and so on.

MILES TO GO

The "odometer" of a car tells you how far it has traveled in its lifetime. The "trip odometer" can be reset at any time to tell you the length of a particular trip. Suppose the main odometer of a new car is at 467 and the trip odometer is at 22. How many miles do you have to travel before the main odometer is precisely two times the trip odometer?

SLIPPERY SLOPES

Brenda the Brave sets off to climb a mountain which is 12,000 feet high. She plans to climb 3,000 feet each day, before taking overnight rests. A mischievous mountain spirit, however, decides to test Brenda's resolve. Each night, Brenda's sleeping bag, with her soundly asleep in it, is magically moved 2,000 feet *back down* the mountain, so that when Brenda awakes in the morning she finds herself only 1,000 feet higher than she was the morning before!

Not one to give up, Brenda eventually succeeds. But how many days does it take her to reach the summit?

THE LONG AND THE SHORT OF THE GRASS

Mr. Greengrass wants his lawn to be tidy and likes the grass cut short. Because he doesn't like mowing but wants to be able sit outside and read the paper on Sunday mornings and be proud of the smooth lawn, he decides to hire some good young mowers.

Two kids agree to mow Mr. Greengrass's grass on Saturdays for 15 weeks. To make sure they come every single Saturday, he agrees to pay them, at the end of the 15 weeks, $2 for every week that they mow it—as long as they will give him $3 for every week they miss.

At the end of the 15 weeks, they owe him exactly as much as he owes them, which is good news for Mr. Greengrass, but a rotten deal for the kids! How many weeks did they miss?

POTATO PAIRS

In Idaho, they proudly say they have giant potatoes, and unusual potato sellers. One of the strangest potato sellers is Potato Mo. She never sells her potatoes one at a time, nor in bags of five or ten pounds. She sells potatoes only in pairs!

One day, Cal the cook wanted a potato that weighed just two pounds, so he went and asked Mo what she had available.

"I have only three potatoes left," she answered. "Here they are: A, B, and C.

"A and B together weigh three pounds; A and C together weigh five pounds; B and C together weigh four pounds. You can have any pair you want."

Can you help Cal the cook buy a pair of potatoes? Which if any of the potatoes weighs two pounds?

CRACKERS!

Mad Marty, crazy as crackers, invites his friends to a cracker puzzle party. The puzzle he sets them is this: How many different kinds of spread can you put on a cracker?

Everyone brings a different kind of spread and Marty supplies a gigantic box of crackers. Then they all get down to business:

Marty has a cracker with mayo =   1 spread

Pete brings peanut butter; so now
   they have: (**1**) mayo, (**2**) peanut
   butter, (**3**) mayo and peanut
   butter =   3 spreads

Jake brings jelly; so now they have
   (**1**) mayo, (**2**) peanut butter,
   (**3**) mayo and peanut butter,
   (**4**) jelly, (**5**) jelly and mayo,
   (**6**) jelly and peanut butter,
   (**7**) jelly and mayo and peanut
   butter =   7 spreads

Hank brings honey =   how many
                                   spreads?

Charlie brings cheese =   how many
                                   spreads?

Fred brings fish-paste =   how many
                                   spreads?

WITCHES' BREW

Three witches were mixing up a dreadful mathematical spell in their cauldron, and one of them—Fat Freddy— was reading out the recipe to the others.

Eye of newt and toe of frog
Wool of bat and tongue of dog

Suddenly they realized they needed some liquid—2 pints of armpit sweat. They had a bucketful of sweat, a saucepan which when full held exactly 3 pints, and a jug which when full held exactly 1 pint. How could they get exactly 2 pints?

Hint   Try filling the pan, and then filling the jug from it.

WITCHES' STEW

Many years later the same witches, now even older and more haggard, were mixing up a super-disgusting stew in their cauldron:

Adder's fork and blind worm's sting
Lizard's leg and howlet's wing...

And once again they needed to add the sweat, mixed this time with tears. They had a bucketful of liquid, and they needed to add exactly 4 pints, but all they had to measure it was a pitcher that held exactly 5 pints and a pot that held exactly 3.

How could they measure out exactly 4 pints?

CYCLOMANIA

In the kids' playground, Donna was delighted to find bicycles with two wheels, and tricycles with, of course, three wheels.

They came in all sorts of different shapes and sizes and colors, but she took a count and discovered that they had 12 wheels altogether.

How many bicycles did Donna find there? And how many tricycles?

COOKIE JARS

Joe and Ken each held a cookie jar and had a look inside them to see how many cookies were left.

Joe said, "If you gave me one of yours, we'd both have the same number of cookies."

Ken said to Joe, "Yes, but you've eaten all yours, and you haven't any left!"

How many cookies does Ken have?

SPRING FLOWERS

On her breakfast tray, Aunt Lily had a little vase of flowers—a mixture of primroses and celandines. She counted up the petals and found there were 39. "Oh, how lovely!" she said, "exactly my age; and the total number of flowers is exactly your age, Rose!"

How old is Rose?

Primroses have five petals on each flower.

Celandines have eight petals on each flower.

FLEABAGS

Two shaggy old dogs were walking down the street.

Captain sits down and scratches his ear, then turns to Champ and growls, "If one of your fleas jumped onto me, we'd have the same number."

Champ barks back, "But if one of yours jumped onto me, I'd have five times as many as you!"

How many fleas are there on Champ?

SQUARES & CUBES

Multiply any number by itself, and you get a square number. So 2 x 2 = 4, and 4 is a square number. And four squares fit together to make a bigger square.

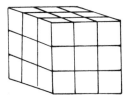

Nine is also a square, because 3 x 3 = 9, and nine squares also fit together to make a bigger square.

Cubes are numbers you get by multiplying a number by itself and then by the same again; so 2 x 2 x 2 = 8, which is a cube.

And 3 x 3 x 3 = 27, another cube. The big cube is made of 27 little cubes.

There is only one 2-digit number (i.e. between 10 and 99) that is both a square and a cube. What is it?

CUBES & SQUARES

There is only one 3-digit number that is both a cube and a square. What is it?

OLD MACDONALD

Old MacDonald had a farm, EE-I-EE-I-OH!
And on that farm he had some pigs, *ee-i-ee-i-oh!*
With an *Oink oink!* here, and an *Oink oink!* there.
Here an *Oink!* There an *Oink!*
Everywhere an *Oink oink!*
Old MacDonald had a farm, EE-I-EE-I-OH!

Old MacDonald had some turkeys, too (certainly with
a *Gobble gobble* here and a *Gobble gobble* there).

One day, while out feeding them all, he noticed that,
if he added everything together, his pigs and his turkeys
had a total of 24 legs and 12 wings between them.

How many pigs did Old MacDonald have? And how
many turkeys?

LOADSALEGS

Two multipedes were dancing together at a party, and trying hard not to trip over each other's feet! One smiled at the other and said, "If you could give me two of your legs we'd have the same number." The other replied, "If I had two of yours, I'd have three times as many legs as you!"

How many legs did each have?

PYRAMIDS

Susie and Ben like to make quick and easy cannonball cookies, so they often make lots and lots.

Today, they decide to heap the cookies up on the table for the family in pyramid shape.

Susie decides to make a triangular base with 6 cookies along each side, and builds up her pyramid from there—5 along each side in the next layer, then 4, then 3, and so on up to 1 on top.

Ben starts by laying out a square on the table, with only 5 cookies on each side. Then he builds up 4 on each side, then 3, and so on.

Which of the two pymamid builders uses more cookies by the time they reach the top?

WRONG ENVELOPE?

You decide one day to write a letter to each of three friends. When you finish, you go to a desk and find three envelopes, write the address on each envelope, and stick on a stamp.

Now, suppose you were to put one letter into each of the envelopes without looking at the front of it, how many ways are there of putting at least one letter into the wrong envelope?

What is the chance that you will get the letters in the right envelopes just by luck?

TRAIN CRASH

There's a single railroad track across the remote desert near the Arizona–New Mexico border. A freight train starts from one end and goes north at 25 mph. An ancient pioneer train starts at the other end and coughs its way south at a mighty 15 mph.

Neither driver sees the other train approaching, and at No Hope Gulch, after both trains have been traveling for exactly one hour, they collide head-on.

There's a lot of arguing about who's to blame, but the question is, How far apart were the trains when they started, exactly one hour before the crash?

SQUISHED FLY

At the moment when the trains started up, a fly that had been sleeping on one locomotive woke up and took off.

Strangely enough, it flew straight up the line at 50 mph to the front of the other train! There, it turned right around and flew straight back to the freight train!

Again, it turned right around and flew *back* to the other train! Backwards and forwards the fly went, between the two trains, until at the bitter end—the fly was *squished* in the crash!

It's a long and strange story, but the question remains: How far did the fly fly, before it died?

HEAVIBRIX

A brick weighs one pound and half a brick. How many pounds do two bricks weigh?

OBJECT PUZZLES

LINE BOGGLERS

Two-Way Street

See if you can make a third arrow that is the same size as the other two by adding only two straight lines.

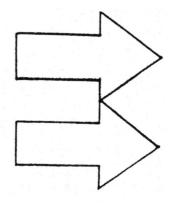

Sum Time

Add two straight lines and divide the clock face into three parts. The sum of the numbers in each part must be the same.

(Two-Way Street) Hint: The new arrow points to the left.

(Sum Time) Hint: The sum of the numbers in each part equals 26.

6+5 = 9???

Can you add five straight lines to these six and get nine?

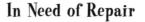

In Need of Repair

Add only one straight line to this equation so that it is correct.

$$1 + 3 + 5 = 148$$

(**In Need of Repair**) **Hint:** Try adding the line to one of the plus signs.

(**6+5 = 9???**) **Hint:** Think about the wording; get NINE.

Tunnels

Try to connect each rectangle with the triangle that has the same number. Lines cannot cross or go outside the diagram.

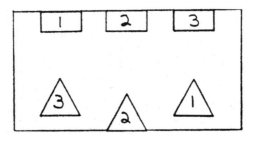

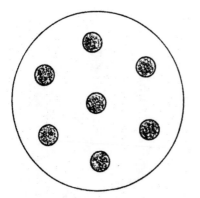

Pepperoni Pizza

Divide the pizza with three straight lines so that there is only one piece of pepperoni on each piece.

(Pepperoni Pizza) Hint: Start with a horizontal line just below the center piece of pepperoni.

(Tunnels) Hint: Connect the two 3s with a straight line.

PENCIL PUZZLES

Can you draw these figures without lifting your pencil off the paper? You are not allowed to retrace any lines but you can cross over lines.

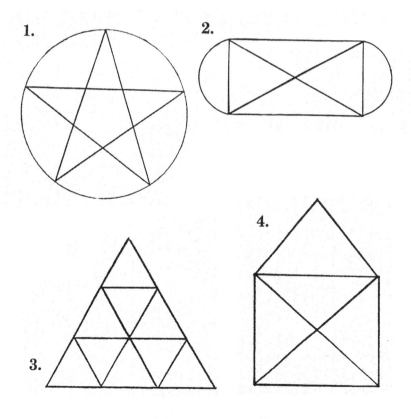

1.

2.

4.

3.

5.

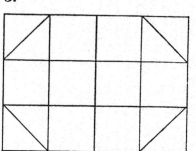

6.

7.

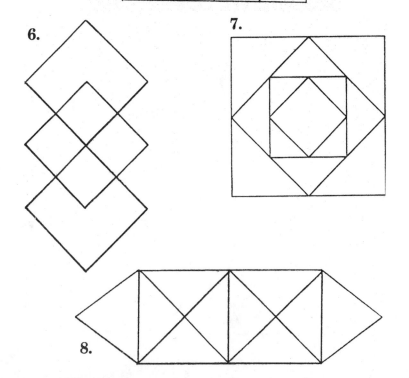

8.

Pencil Puzzles Secret

Look at these points where the lines meet. They are called vertices (pronounced ver-tis-sees). Odd vertices have an odd number of lines that meet at the point.

Examples

Odd Vertices

Leonard Euler (pronounced "oiler"), a famous Swiss mathematician, discovered that a figure can only be traced if it has 0 or 2 odd vertices. If the figure has 0 odd vertices, start at any point and finish at the same point. If a figure has 2 odd vertices, start at one point and finish at the other.

TOOTHPICK TEASERS

Architect

Build a house using 11 toothpicks as shown in the diagram. See if you can make the house face the opposite direction by moving only one toothpick.

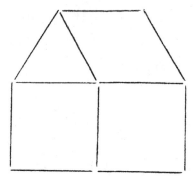

Crisscross

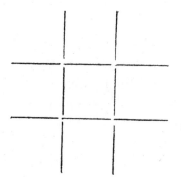

Arrange 12 toothpicks as shown in the diagram. Can you move only three toothpicks and end up with exactly three congruent squares?

(Architect) Hint: Move one of the toothpicks in the roof.

(Crisscross) Hint: Start by moving the bottom-left toothpick.

Aquarium

Make a fish using eight toothpicks and a coin as shown in the diagram. Move only three toothpicks and the coin so that the fish is swimming to the right.

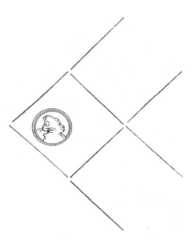

Square Deal

The toothpicks in this diagram have been arranged to form squares. Can you remove two of the toothpicks so that only two squares remain?

(Aquarium) Hint: Start by moving the bottom tail toothpick.

(Square Deal) Hint: Do the squares have to be congruent?

In and Out

The four toothpicks in this diagram represent a wine glass with a coin inside. See if you can move two toothpicks so that the coin is *outside* the glass.

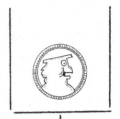

Equilateral Triangles

Arrange 16 toothpicks as shown in the diagram. Remove four toothpicks so that only four triangles remain.

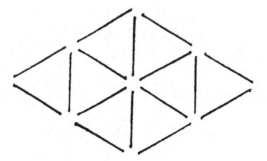

(Equilateral Triangles) Hint: Do all the triangles have to be congruent?

(In and Out) Hint: The glass will be upside down.

COIN BAFFLERS

Over Easy

Can you make the left triangle look like the right triangle by moving only three coins?

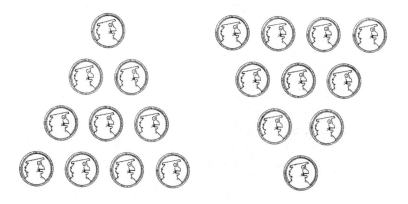

Four Across

Arrange six coins in the shape of a
cross. There are four coins in one
direction and three coins in the
other. Try to move only one coin
so that there are four coins in each
direction.

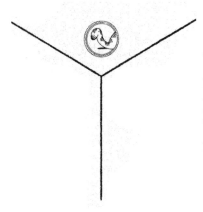

Do Not Touch

This is a drawing of a coin
inside a martini glass. Can
you remove the coin from
the glass without touching
the glass or the coin?

(Do Not Touch) Hint: Look at the glass from a different angle.

(Four Across) Hint: Move the bottom coin.

Constellation

Draw a constellation puzzle on a piece of paper. Make it much larger than the diagram so that four coins can freely move from one circle to the next. Put two like coins on circles 2 and 8, and put two other like coins on circles 4 and 6.

The object is to make the two top coins change places with the two bottom coins by sliding them, one at a time, along the lines from circle to circle. You can slide a coin as many times as you like, but coins can only be moved to open circles.

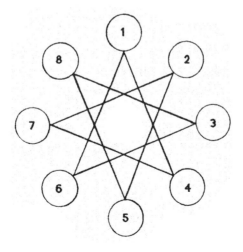

Hint: Start by moving 2 to 7. Then move 8 to 5 to 2.

Coin Checkers

Draw a coin checker puzzle on a piece of paper. Make it large enough so that four coins can freely move from space to space. Place the four coins on the puzzle as shown in the diagram, heads on the left and tails on the right.

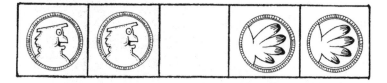

   See if you can make the heads and tails change places. The moves for this puzzle are like the moves in checkers. You can slide any coin to an open space next to it, or you can jump any coin over the coin next to it into an open space. The record for this puzzle is 8 moves. If it takes you more than *8 moves*, keep trying and see if you can get it.

Hint: Start by moving a heads into the empty space and then jump it with a tails.

NUMBER JUGGLING

Box Score

Use each of the numbers from 1 through 8. See if you can put a different number in each box so that no two consecutive numbers are touching—*not even at their corners*. For example, the box with the 5 cannot touch the box with the 4 or 6.

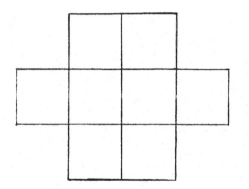

Wheel Numbers

Use each of the numbers from 1 through 9. Put a different number in each circle so that the sum of each straight row of three circles is 15.

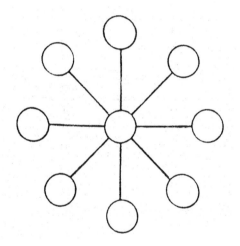

Bermuda Triangle

Use each of the numbers from 1 through 9. Can you put a different number in each circle so that the sum of each side of the triangle is 17?

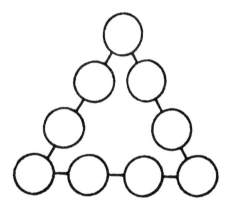

Troublesum

Use each of the numbers from 1 through 9. See if you can put a different number in each box so that the total is 900.

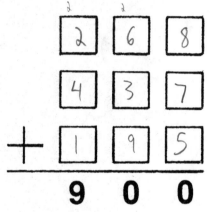

Riddle Me

How many feet are in a yard?

Magic Square

Use each of the numbers from 1 through 9. Can you put a different number in each box so that the sum of each row, column, and diagonal is 15?

(**Magic Square**) **Hint:** Find the center number first.

Hexagram

Use each of the numbers from 1 through 12. Put a different number in each circle so that the sum of each straight row of four circles is 26. Four numbers have been filled in to get you started.

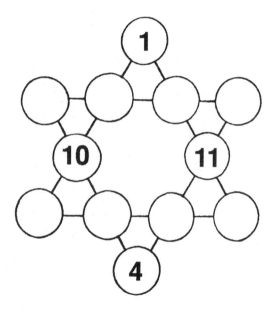

BRAIN BUSTERS

Stargazer

See if you can draw this figure without lifting your pencil off the paper. You are not allowed to retrace any lines but can cross over lines.

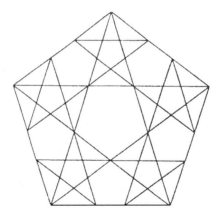

Hint: There are no odd vertices, so start at any point and finish at that same point.

Box Score II

Use each of the numbers from 1 through 12. Put a different number in each box so that no two consecutive numbers are touching—*not even at their corners.* For example, the box with the 11 cannot touch the box with the 10 or the 12.

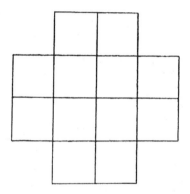

Windowpanes

Arrange 12 toothpicks as shown in the diagram. Can you move only four toothpicks and end up with exactly ten squares? No, you cannot break any toothpicks in half!

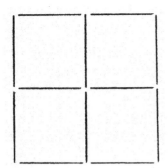

Dot To Dot

Try to connect all nine dots using only four straight lines. Lines can cross, but you cannot lift your pencil off the paper or retrace any lines.

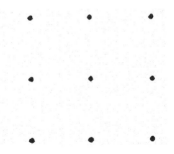

(Dot To Dot) Hint: Try not to picture a square in your mind. See only dots and empty space.

(Windowpanes) Hint: Do all the squares have to be congruent?

Riddle Me 11

Why is the U.S. nickel coin smarter than the penny?

Tunnels 11

See if you can connect each square with the triangle that has the same number. Lines cannot cross or go outside the diagram.

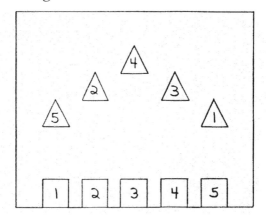

(**Tunnels 11**) **Hint:** Connect the two 2's with a straight line.

Tetrahedron

Can you think of a way to make *four* triangles,
all the *same size* as those shown below, with
only six toothpicks?

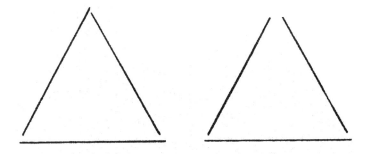

FUNNY BUSINESS

FUNNY BUSINESS

Here are some silly pranks that you can use to fool your family, friends, and math teacher. These amusing tricks can be performed by themselves or used as follow-up jokes when someone asks you to repeat some other trick. Either way, they will be a lot of fun for everyone!

I'VE GOT 11 FINGERS!?!

Your friends will think that they have lost their minds when you prove to them that you have eleven fingers!

Hold up both of your hands in front of your friend and ask, "How many fingers do you see?" She, of course, will say, "10."

You reply, "10? Let's see." Count backwards from 10, one finger at a time, on your right hand. Then add the five fingers on your left hand and you will get a total of 11 fingers!

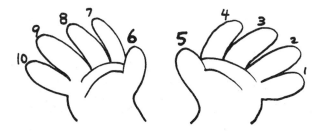

"10, 9, 8, 7, **6**, plus **5** on my left hand equals **11**!?!"

MULTIPLICATION MADNESS

Did you know that 6 x 5 = 8 x 4? Your friends won't believe it either, but you can prove it to them. Here's how.

6 x 5 = 30 and 8 x 4 = 32 (it's 30 too!)

SIMPLE MATH

I + 9 + I + 9 + I

Give your friend exactly 30 seconds to figure out what simple operation can be performed on these numbers so that they will equal 15. Tell him that he cannot cross off or add any new numbers. It's easy. Just turn the page upside down!

FAST TALKER

Your friends will be amazed when you count up to 500 in only five seconds! Tell them that you will start at one and count by ones, one number at a time. Count very quickly up to twenty as an example. Explain that in exactly five seconds, you will count up to a number between four and five hundred. Be careful that you don't say, "between four *hundred* and five hundred." Have a friend time you, and when she says "Go," just count up to ten. After all, 10 is between 4 and 500!

LOWEST TERMS

Here's a much easier way to reduce fractions. You don't even have to divide. Ask your math teacher if you can reduce all your fractions this way!

Example

Reduce $\dfrac{8}{14}$

Warning: Don't try this on a test unless your math teacher has a *great* sense of humor!

HALF AND HALF

Hand your friend a dollar and tell her that she can have it if she can fold it in half seven times. Don't worry about losing that dollar. No matter how hard your friend tries, she will not be able to make that seventh fold.

The Secret

The dollar will be half as big every time it is folded. So, after the sixth fold, it will be very small and hard to handle. Also, the number of layers doubles with every fold. After six folds, your friend will be trying to fold 64 layers of paper!

RIDICULOUS REDUCING

$$\frac{1\cancel{9}}{\cancel{9}5} = \frac{1}{5} \qquad \frac{1\cancel{6}}{\cancel{6}4} = \frac{1}{4} \qquad \frac{2\cancel{6}}{\cancel{6}5} = \frac{2}{5} \qquad \frac{4\cancel{9}}{\cancel{9}8} = \frac{4}{8} = \frac{1}{2}$$

Warning: These four fractions are special cases and this ridiculous method of reducing only works for them! If you reduce the fractions on your homework this way, you will get them all wrong!

CALCULATOR RIDDLES

CALCULATOR RIDDLES

The calculator that you own is a remarkable little machine. You've always known that it can perform mathematical calculations faster and with more accuracy than most humans, but did you know that it can also talk?

Yes, it's true! Your calculator will talk to you if you push the right buttons. For example, your calculator will tell you its name if you push "clear" and then *carefully* push **353 x 9 x 100 + 18 =**. Just turn the calculator *upside down*, and it will tell you!

Now that you and your calculator have been properly introduced, it's time to have some fun! Use the calculator alphabet below to help you find the answers to the math jokes and riddles in this section. If you don't understand an answer, look at the explanation in the back of the book or just ask your calculator!

The Calculator Alphabet

Upside-down numbers: 0 1 2 3 4 5 6 7 8 9
Letters: O I Z E h S g L B G

1. What is the only thing that gets larger the more you take away?

25,000 − 68 − 952 − 8,956 − 11,320 =

2. Which has fewer legs, a goose or no goose?

25.009 / .001 + 10,000 =

3. Picture these U.S. coins: a nickel, a penny, and a dime. OK? Ellie's parents have 3 children. One is Nick and another is Penny. Who is the third?

.05 / .01 / .10 x 3 x 211 + 123 =

4. How many legs does a barbershop quartet have?

2 x 2 x 2 x 10 x 70 + 338 − .09 =

5. A pet store owner has 17 eels. All but 9 were sold. How many eels does the owner have left?

$$337.8 \times 17 - 9 =$$

6. Who weighs more, Lee the 5-foot (152 cm) butcher or Bob the 7-foot (213 cm) wrestler?

$$5 \times 7 \times 10 - 13 =$$

7. A doctor gave you three pills and said to take one every half hour. How long will the pills last?

$$3 \times .5 + 2.6 =$$

8. Which would you rather halve, an old one-hundred-dollar bill or a brand-new one?

100 x 77 + 118.001 – 100 =

9. Bob and Bill took a diving test in school. Bob wore glasses and Bill did not. Who got a higher score on the test?

10 x 10 x 10 – 200 + 8 =

10. How many seconds are in a year?

31,557,600 / 1,000,000 – 26.3476 =

11. A barrel of water weighed 100 kilograms, but after somebody put something in it, it weighed only 25 kilograms. What was put in the barrel?

500 x 100 + 4,000 – 300 + 4 =

12. Bill subtracted numbers for 20 minutes, Bess multiplied them, and Leslie added them.

Who was more exhausted when they finished?

9 + 57 + 868 + 7,920 + 93,208 + 215,475 =

Who went into debt when they were finished?

17,865 – 9,438 – 607 – 95 – 7 =

Who got the most work done in 20 minutes?

.3 x 2 x 2.6 x 20 x 7.1 x 25 =

13. What number did the math teacher bring the student who fainted?

222 x .2 / 2 - .2 – 20 =

14. What is the largest number that will fit in your calculator's display?

99,999,999 / 9 – 11,058,162 + 656,060 =

15. Bob says that only one month has 28 days. His boss says that there are more. Who is right?

28 x 29 x 30 + 31 – 18,882.486 =

16. What did the seven do that made all the other numbers afraid of it?

7 x .07 /.7 x 7 + 1.9 =

17. What number never tells the truth when it is resting?

223,314 / 7 / 2 / 3 =

18. How much dirt is in a hole that is 5-feet deep, 2-feet wide, and 3-feet long?

5 x 2 x 3 – 30 =

19. Take two eggs from three eggs and what do you have?

9,992 x .2 x 3 – 2 =

20. What part of a lame dog reminds you of what happens when you start adding 37 and 26?

224 x 25 – 25.486 + 37 + 26 =

THINK TANK ANSWERS

Easier by the Dozen

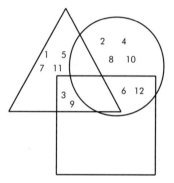

Magic Circle

If you group the numbers as shown below, you can see that the sum of the numbers in each group equals 15. (4 + 5 + 6 = 15; 7 + 8 = 15; 9 + 1 + 2 + 3 = 15)

Eggs-actly

Did you check the hint to see that it was a trick question? If the pot of water is big enough, four eggs can all be boiled at the same time, so it takes three and a half minutes to boil four eggs—same as with just one!

Just Checking

Each of the five kids plays four games, so it looks as though there must have been 5 x 4 = 20 games played in all. But wait! The game that Simon played against Theodore (for example) is the same game that Theodore played against Simon. You can't count the games twice. The actual number of games played equals 20/2 = 10 games.

Looking at it another way, suppose the first player plays each of the others, for a total of 4 games. Then the second player plays the 3 remaining players (other than player #1), and so on. You get a total of 4 + 3 + 2 + 1 = 10 games.

The One and Only

Forty is the number, as you can plainly see.

A B C D E **F** G H I J K L M
N **O** P Q **R** S **T** U V W X **Y** Z

Letter Perfect

ELEVEN PLUS TWO can be rearranged to spell TWELVE PLUS ONE!

Countdown

There are 9 rectangles altogether: four small ones (A, B, C, and D), four that you get by putting the smaller ones together (A-B, A-C, B-D, and C-D), and of course the big one, A-B-C-D.

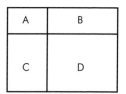

Square Route

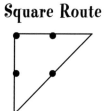

No Honor Among Thieves

None of the three visitors is guilty.

If the Scarecrow were guilty, then his statement that the Tin Man was innocent would be false, so the Tin Man would also be guilty, but that cannot be the case. Similarly, the Tin Man can't be guilty, because otherwise the Cowardly Lion would also be guilty. And since the Tin Man must be innocent, his statement about the Cowardly Lion being innocent must be true. Therefore none of the three is guilty, just as it should be!

Circular Reasoning

Line C divides the circle into two equal pieces. It is the only line that goes through the center of the circle.

Connect the Dots

A five-pointed star does the trick.

Pickup Sticks

TWENTY NINE = 29

Long Division

Cover up the left half of the figure 8 below. What's left looks a lot like a 3, doesn't it?

When in Rome

Now cover up the bottom half of the figure below, which

happens to be 9, in Roman numerals. What's left should give you 4, also in Roman numerals.

Number Path

6	7	10	11	12
5	8	9	14	13
4	1	20	15	16
3	2	19	18	17

Seeing Is Believing?

This problem is a bit of an optical illusion. The answer is line A, even though line B, at first glance, appears to be correct.

Diamond in the Rough

The only diamond that is not symmetrical is the seven of diamonds.

Three's a Charm

The item costs 17 cents. To purchase it requires four coins: one dime, one nickel, and two pennies. To purchase two items (34 cents) requires six coins: one quarter, one nickel, and four pennies. To purchase three items (51 cents) requires only two coins: one half-dollar and one penny.

Who Is the Liar?

Daniel is the liar. To see why, we examine one case at a time, using the fact that only one person is lying.

If Andrew were lying, the number would have three digits. (It couldn't have just one digit, because then it couldn't be divisible by 25, and Daniel would also be lying.) But if the number had three digits, either Barbara or Cindy would have to be lying, because 150 is the only three-digit number that goes evenly into 150. Therefore Andrew must be telling the truth, because there can only be one liar.

If Barbara were lying, then the number does not go into 150. But then either Andrew or Daniel must be lying, because the only two-digit numbers that are divisible by 25 (25, 50, and 75) all go evenly into 150. So Barbara must be telling the truth.

If Cindy were lying, then the number would be 150. But then Andrew would also have to be lying, because 150 has three digits, not two. And we know Andrew is telling the truth.

So, the only possibility left is that Daniel is the liar, and this works out. If the number were 10, for example, Daniel would be lying, but the other three statements would all be true.

No Foolin'

April 1, 2001 is a Sunday. That's because one year is 365 days, or 52 weeks and one day. Any date moves ahead one day from year to year.

However, in a leap year, any date after February 29 moves ahead two days. The year 2000 was a leap year, so April 1, 1999 must have been a Thursday.

Square Dance

By taking out the four segments in the middle of the diagram, you reduce the number of squares from eighteen to nine (eight small squares and one big one).

Please Fence Me In

If you make the pen in the shape of a circle, you will get the biggest area for a given amount of fencing.

Prime Time

The only one of the first ten primes that is left out of the original diagram is the number 7. But, as you can see, it makes an appearance if you shade in all the other primes.

32	16	24	33	45	28	54
40	23	2	11	5	19	12
14	36	10	55	17	34	49
6	50	38	13	22	51	20
21	35	3	46	27	18	39
9	29	48	15	4	52	26
55	44	25	8	42	30	1

Pieces of Eight

Each point from A to H (the "vertices" of the octagon) can be connected with five other points to form a diagonal. That seems to make a total of 8 x 5, or 40 diagonals. However, as it said in the hint, the diagonal from A to E is the same as the diagonal from E to A, and you can't double-count. You need to divide 40 by 2 to get the actual answer—20 diagonals.

On the Trail
1,009 in Roman numerals is MIX. It is the only number that is a common English word in Roman numerals.

Spreading the Word
Four dimes are enough. Pages 30 and 31 are on the same spread, and because it is a pocket dictionary and therefore a small size, they could easily be copied on the same sheet.

The Big Inning of the End
The game was played in Los Angeles. The key is that the most runs a team can score at any given moment is four—a grand slam. If the game had been played in Houston, it would have been over as soon as Houston, the home team, got the lead in the tenth inning. In other words, it is impossible for the home team to win by more than four runs in an extra inning game.

From Start to Finish
The total number of trips from S (Start) to F (Finish) equals 10. The easiest way to solve the problem is to use the diagram and count them up!

For a more systematic way to arrive at the answer, we start by observing that at each point you have a choice between moving across or moving down. Altogether you have to move across three times and down twice in order to get from S to F. So a pattern that would get you from S to F might look something like AADAD, where A means across and D means down.

Using our notation of A's and D's, the ten patterns are as follows:

AAADD   ADAAD
AADAD   DDAAA
AADDA   DADAA
ADDAA   DAAAD
ADADA   DAADA

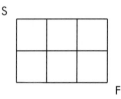

How Big?

Note that the big square is divided into nine pieces: one square, four small triangles, and four odd-shaped four-sided figures (called trapezoids). Each of the four small triangles, when put together with one of the trapezoids, forms a triangle whose two pieces can easily be rearranged to form a square with the same area as the central square. Since there are a total of five identical squares, the central square is therefore one-fifth the area of the larger one.

The Birthday Surprise

The professor had forgotten that the class included a pair of identical twins! (This is apparently a true story, the professor in question being famed logician and author Raymond Smullyan.)

Not Just Any Word Will Do

The five other words are bow, box, boy, cow, and coy.

The Run-Off

Burt will win. Why? Because when the two of them ran against Alex, Burt was exactly 20 meters ahead of Carl at the moment Alex crossed the finish line. Therefore, if Burt were to give Carl a 20-meter head start, they will be even at that point. But that point is 20 meters from the finish line, and Burt is the faster runner. Therefore he would win the race—but not by much!

Staying in Shape

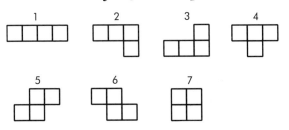

Mirror Time

The answer is 49 minutes, the time between 12:12 and 1:01.

One of a Kind

The number is four.

Whose Side Are You On?

Altogether there are 10 changes of sides, five per set—after the 1st, 3rd, 5th, 7th, and 9th games. Because 10 is an even number, the two players must have ended up on the same sides at which they began the match.

Win One for the Dipper

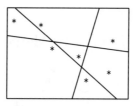

Going Crackers

The junior employee argued that what the survey said was 1) Crackers are better than nothing, and 2) Nothing is better than peanuts. Putting the two together, you get that crackers are better than peanuts!

Five Easy Pieces

It's a trick question, of course. A square can be divided into any number of equal parts simply by drawing vertical or horizontal lines!

It's in the Bag

Pick the second bag. The second bag gives you a 2/3 chance of picking a red marble, while the chance of a red marble from the first bag is only 3/5. (To see that 2/3 is greater than 3/5, find the common denominator of 15: 2/3 = 10/15, while 3/5 = 9/15.)

Switching Sides

The greatest number of sides you can have is 7. The diagram shows two ways of reaching this total. (There are many other solutions, some of which are simply rotations of the solutions above. Others involve sides consisting of more than one segment—for example, if you pushed out either lower diagonal of the right-hand figure, you would get a seven-sided figure with a squared-off corner.)

The Missing Shekel

The problem with the price of five rutabagas for two shekels is that the five rutabagas consist of 3 cheap ones (the three for a shekel variety) and 2 expensive ones (the neighbor's two for a shekel batch). By selling the combined 60 rutabagas in this manner, the farmer is basically selling 40 at his price and 20 at his neighbor's more expensive price—not 30 at each price. That's why he ends up a shekel short.

What Do They Play?

A: Stacy gave the soccer player a ride to the last game.

B: The chess player said that Stacy drives too fast.

C: Meredith went to the prom with the chess player's brother.

A) means that Stacy isn't the soccer player. B) means that Stacy isn't the chess player. Therefore Stacy plays golf.

C) means that Meredith isn't the chess player, so she must be the soccer player. That leaves Alex as the chess player.

Class Dismissed

The fourth period will end at 11:55, or five minutes before noon. That's because the four class periods take up 4 x 40 = 160 minutes, while there are a total of 15 minutes between periods. That's 175 minutes in all, which is just five minutes less than 180 minutes, which is three hours.

Quarter Horses

B is shortest, A is in the middle, and C is longest. Note that A is just the radius of the circle, while B is clearly shorter than the radius. As for C, you can see from the picture below that the fence is longer than the radius. So, if C is longer than A, and B is shorter than A, you have your answer: B is the shortest and C is the longest.

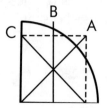

And Then There Was One

The only letter left standing is the letter W.

Does Gold Glitter?

Tracy is probably right, because the expression "All that glitters is not gold" is supposed to mean that gold isn't the only thing that glitters. However, Sean has a good point. What he noticed was that if "all that glitters" means "everything that glitters," then it looks as though everything that glitters is not gold, which makes it look like there are many things that glitter, but that gold doesn't happen to be one of them!

It's probably best to stick with Tracy's version and not lose sleep over this one!

Four of a Kind

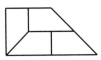

Hex-a-Gone

To create a cube, separate the figure into three diamond-shaped pieces. To see the cube, just tilt your head!

X Marks the Spot

The gray squares show two ways to add five new X's so that every row and column has an even number of X's.

All in Black and White

The number of seasons in a year = 4.

The number of planets in the solar system = 9.

The number of cards in a complete deck = 52.

4 x 9 + 52 = 88, which happens to be the number of keys on a piano.

Sweet Sixteen

Here is the missing snowman. He seems happy that you found him!

Magic Triangle

Here is one solution. Other solutions may be obtained by rotating this one to change the positions of the numbers, but the position of the numbers in relation to one another doesn't change.

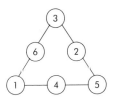

An Updated Classic

You can either add to the original diagram and create four squares, as in the left diagram, or you can separate the original shape into four identical, smaller shapes.

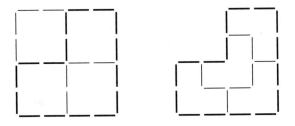

Eight Is Enough

Here are the eight patterns:

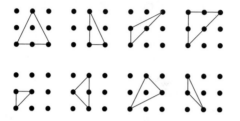

Where's Waldo?

Waldo's position must be as shown in the diagram. Because each row has the same number of students, they must fill up the entire 5 x 6 rectangle, for 30 students in all.

The Christmas Carolers

Believe it or not, the journey must end at house E. House E is the only other house with an *odd* number of paths leading from it. It is not possible to start at any house other than A or E and make a "closed loop" of the type the Christmas carolers set out to do.

Forever Young

The most likely explanation is that Heather was born in Australia, New Zealand or some other place in the Southern Hemisphere, where it is winter during the months that are summer for the Northern Hemisphere. That way she could have been born in, say, July, which means that she wouldn't have reached her 40th birthday as of April 2006.

All in the Family

There are five kids in the family: four boys and one girl. Each of the brothers has a sister, all right—but it's the same one!

Squaring the Circle

When you join the diagonals of the tilted square, you divide the outside square into four smaller squares. But precisely one-half of each of these smaller squares is contained inside the tilted square, so the tilted square must be half the size of the outside square.

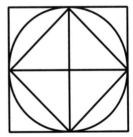

Too Close for Comfort

The figure below is one solution. Another can be obtained by interchanging the two outer "columns." In either case, the middle boxes are occupied by the "1" and the "8."

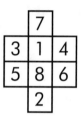

Prime Territory

The only number that satisfies both conditions is 735.

Stay Out of My Path!

Here is one solution: Any other solutions use the same idea—you need to "wrap" two paths around one of the middle squares in order to keep from crossing lines.

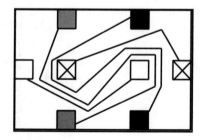

Hundred's Place

The number 100 is found at the base of a tall column.
Note that 96 is a multiple of 6, and all the multiples of 6 are
located in the top spot of one of the tall columns. From there
you just count a few more until getting to the magic 100.

Occupational Hazards

We know that Mr. Carpenter is not a potter (because the
puzzle says so), and we also know that Mr. Carpenter cannot
be a carpenter, because no one's job matches his name.
Therefore Mr. Carpenter is a baker. We also know that Mr.
Potter cannot be a potter, so Mr. Baker must be the potter,
which leaves Mr. Potter as the carpenter.

As for young Mr. Baker, he is hired by one of the men other
than his father. He cannot work for Mr. Carpenter, because he
cannot be a baker. That means that he works for Mr. Potter;
because Mr. Potter is a carpenter, young Mr. Baker must also
be a carpenter!

Straightening It Out

There are two copies of piece G in the rectangle.

Number Ghost

The chain is 2681, 1235, 5706, 6885, 5342.

Last Train to Clarksville

It is now 4:39. Brian has to wait 9 minutes for his train (to
Newburgh). Amy has to wait 18 minutes for her train (to

Springfield), while Stephanie has to wait 36 minutes for her train (to Clarksville).

Crossing the Bridge

The one ace, three 7's, two 5's, and two 4's account for eight cards, so you only have five left (each hand has 13 cards). The greatest number of points you could have from those five cards would be 18—three aces (you already have one) and two kings. If you add those 18 points to the 4 points for the ace you already have, you would have a total of 22 points.

Showing Your Age

Richard and Sylvia's statements were consistent with one another, so either they were both telling the truth or both were lying. But if at least one of them was lying, then they both were. (We'll forgive them. It's their party, after all.) That means that Sylvia is older than Richard.

Test Patterns

The 3 x 3 square makes an appearance in the lower left section of the 9 x 9 square.

Cookie Monster

Elmo's and Peter's chances are both 1/3. Clearly this is true for Elmo, because when he chooses there are three cookies, only one of which is a sugar cookie. By the time Peter chooses his cookie, he will only have a chance at the sugar cookie in two out of three cases—when Elmo hasn't already picked it! But of those two occasions in three, Peter's chance at getting the sugar cookie will be 1/2, and 2/3 times 1/2 equals 1/3. Another way to think of the puzzle is this: Suppose there was a third person—Max—who went *after* Elmo and Peter. Clearly Max will get the sugar cookie whenever it is the only one left, and the chances of that happening must be 1/3. But if Elmo's chances are 1/3 and Max's chances are 1/3, the same must be true for Peter—after all, someone must get the sugar cookie!

The End Is in Sight

Suppose you start by moving to the H on the left. If you then move to the E on the left, you must then move to the E in the middle to begin the word END, at which point you have two choices for N. While if you move to the E in the center, you have two choices for the E that begins END, and only one choice for N. That's four paths if you start with the H on the left, and, using the same reasoning, you also get four paths if you start with the H on the right. Altogether, that's eight ways of saying THE END.

Gloves Galore!

This is trickier than the socks, because some gloves fit on the right hand and some on the left. You *might* pick out all 12 left hand gloves, one right after the other, but then the next must make a pair; so you need to take 13 gloves to make sure.

The Wolf, the Goat, and the Cabbage

Take the goat across. Go back; take the wolf across, and bring the goat back. Take the cabbage across. Go back for the goat. Then the goat is never alone with either the wolf or the cabbage.

Nine Coins

She set up the coins as shown. Can you find the rows now? Let's count them.

The 3-coin rows are:
3 rows across (top, middle
and bottom), 4 diagonal (two
one way two the other,
1 down the middle, and...
2 *long* diagonals criss-crossing through the center!

Eight Coins

The secret is to start with #4 and move it onto #7— or start with #5 and move it onto #2. Then it's reasonably easy; try it and see. (If you want the whole solution: move #4 to #7, #6 to #2, #1 to #3, and #5 to #8.) Remember—a pile of two coins counts as two to jump over!

Odd Balls

Yes, this can be done, but you have to put at least one bag inside of another. You could put 3 balls in each of 3 bags, and then one of these bags inside the fourth bag. Or you could put all the balls in bag 1, put that in bag 2, put that in bag 3, and put the whole lot in bag 4. And there are many others!

Tricky Connections

No, it can't be done. The connections are impossible without allowing one line to cross another, using a bridge, or by putting a line under a house!

Cube of Cheese

You have to make one cut to make each face of the cube; so however you pile the pieces, you must make six cuts in all.

Crate Expectations

There are many different patterns that work, but here is an easy one to remember.

Now try ten bottles!

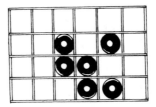

The Pizza and the Sword

To get the maximum number of pieces you must make sure that each cut crosses all the previous cuts, but not at old crossings. If all three cuts cross in the middle, you can get only 6 pieces, but if you keep the crossings separate you get 7.

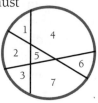

Pencil Squares

From the puzzle, remove the top middle pencil and two lower-left corner pencils.

Pencil Triangles

What you have to do is build them into a 3-dimensional pyramid, with a triangle on each of its three sides, and *one underneath*.

The Rolling Quarter

Twice. Try it and see.

Sliding Quarters

Use the dark quarter to push the other ones in the direction of the arrows.

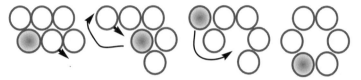

Practice this before you try to show anyone!

Find the Gold

Ask to see a sample from the box labeled MIXTURE, because you know it isn't one. If it's gold, that box must be full of gold; take it. If the sample is of iron, then take the box labeled IRON, because you know the gold is in neither the GOLD nor the MIXTURE.

Frisky Frogs

Freda steps, Fred hops over her, Frank steps, Freda hops, Francine hops, Fergie steps, Fred hops, Frank hops, Frambo hops, Freda steps, Francine hops, Fergie hops, Frank steps, Frambo hops, Fergie steps—and they are all across, in 15 moves.

Leaping Lizards

Try using these guide rules: 1. Don't move a boy next to another boy—or a girl next to another girl—until you reach the other side; 2. Step if you can, hop if you can't step;

3. Once you have moved a girl, keep moving girls till you have to stop; then move boys till you have to stop. The quickest has 23 leaps.

Picnic Mystery

The cake isn't in the CAKE box, and it can't be in the COOKIE box, because that's the only place for the fruit; so it must be in the box labeled FRUIT.

Wiener Triangles

You can make 5 triangles, including the big one round the outside.

Tennis Tournament

In a knockout tournament, every player has to lose one match —except the winner, who loses none. So the total number of matches is one less than the number of players. If 27 enter, there will be 26 matches.

Magic Hexagon

Make sure the middle number, in this case 4, is in the center.

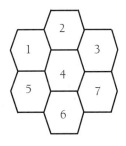

Three Sisters

Charlie's wife isn't the builder, and she isn't the cook (or the first letters would match); so she must be the architect, and she must be Beadie, or the first letters would match. Therefore Cedie can't be the architect or the cook; she must be the builder, and be married to Mr. Able. And so the cook, married to Dr. Baker, must be Ady.

The Power of Seven

After 4 have been killed, and there are 20 left, the commander must put 2 in each corner tower, and 3 along each side wall.

Bundles of Tubes

These are the shapes formed by bundles of tubes naturally, starting with 1 and then making hexagons of 6, 12, and 18:

1 tube + 6 = 7 tubes   + 12 = 19 tubes   + 18 = 37 tubes

  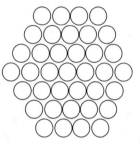

House Colors

Houses #1 and #3 must be green, because they are not next door to one another; so Bernice and her family live in the middle house.

Three J's

Joan is 32; Jane is 28; Jean is 16.

Cutting the Horseshoe

First cut across both arms, leaving two holes below the cut on each side, to give three pieces. (Cut 1)

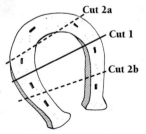

Pile these up so that your second cut snips each of the bottom ends in half, and cuts out the top section with one hole. (Cut 2)

You have seven holey pieces!

No Burglers

Start in the kitchen, and go first through either door #6 or door #10; then you will find the rest easy.

Puzzle of the Sphinx

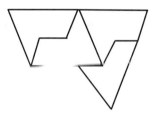

Perforation!

Tear the sheet in a zigzag pattern, starting from the left, one stamp up from the bottom. Then slide the lower piece up to the right.

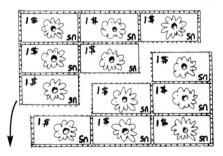

Wild Geese

A square inside a square will do it!

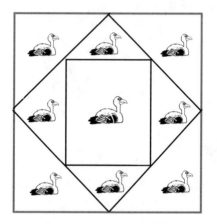

Beefy Bison

Colored Balls #1

One possible solution:

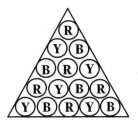

Logical Pop

You should shake either the can labeled MILK SHAKE or the can labeled POP. The potato chips must be in one of those two cans, and they should rattle.

Suppose you shake the MILK SHAKE can; if it rattles it contains the chips; the pop must be in the can labeled POTATO CHIPS.

If it doesn't rattle, it must contain the pop.

Meanwhile if you shake the pop can and it rattles, the chips must be in it; so the milk shake must be in the can labeled POTATO CHIPS, which means the pop must be in the MILK SHAKE can. If it doesn't rattle, the pop must be in the can labeled POTATO CHIPS.

How Many Ducks?

She may have seen only three ducks.

Pool of Glue

Peony says it was Petal; Petal says it was not. These two statements claim opposite things; so one of them must be true and one must be a lie.

Since two of the girls are telling the truth, the third statement—Pansy's—must be true. So Pansy is telling the truth, which means that Peony did it.

Upending the Cups

The secret is to turn one cup back upside-down on your second move. So, for example, turn 1, 2, and 3; then turn 3, 4, and 5; and finally turn 3, 6, and 7.

Puzzling Sand

Bill put the 5-pound weight in one box and balanced it with sand. Then he took the weight out, and balanced the sand with 5 pounds of sand in the other box. Then he put the 5 pound weight on top of the sand in one box, and the 4 pound weight in the other, and balanced up; so now one box had 6 pounds of sand, and the other 5. Finally he took both weights out, and put the 5 pound weight on top of the six pounds of sand. Then when he had balanced that, he knew he had exactly 11 pounds of sand.

Secret Number Codes

For each letter look at the number in the table, and add 1. So A=2, B=3, C=4, etc. The message reads MEET ME AT SEVEN.

Sweet Spot

Wendy said to herself, "Suppose I'm a black spot." Now, think about what Windy sees *if Wendy is black*. He sees one black spot and one white. He thinks, "If I were black, then Woody would see two black spots, and would know he was white."

But Woody has not jumped up; so this cannot be true; Windy cannot be black. So Windy must know that he is white.

But Windy has not jumped up and said so. Therefore Wendy's first guess must be wrong; Wendy cannot be black; so she *knows* she is white—and being the quickest to figure it out, she deserves to win the candy.

TRICKY ARITHMETIC ANSWERS

Waiting in Line

It's easy to guess 14, but the actual answer is 15 customers. To see why, suppose that only numbers 17, 18, and 19 were waiting. Now 19 - 17 = 2, but clearly there are three customers, not two. The general rule is that you must subtract the two numbers and then add one.

Who Is Faster?

Hector can run a mile in eight minutes, so it takes him 64 minutes to run eight miles. But Darius can run eight miles in just 60 minutes, so Darius is faster. There could be another question here. Could Hector keep up his eight-minute pace for an entire hour? Maybe, maybe not. However, if he can't keep it up, it proves that Darius is even faster!

The Average Student

Three five-star homework papers will do the trick. Altogether they account for 3 x 5 = 15 stars. Adding the single star from the first homework gives 16 stars from four assignments, for an average of four stars per assignment.

Looking at the problem another way, note that the one-star homework paper was three stars under the desired average of four stars. Each five-star homework gains one point on the average, so it takes three of them to balance things out.

Big Difference

The biggest possible difference is as follows:

Not Such a Big Difference

If we want the smallest possible difference instead, that would be:

Short Division

$$
\begin{array}{r}
71{,}091{,}051 \\
7\overline{\smash)497{,}637{,}357}
\end{array}
$$

The number 497,637,357 can be broken up into six pieces—49-7-63-7-35-7—each of which is divisible by 7. If you divide the five pieces one by one and then put them together, you get the answer shown above.

The Missing Six

There is more than one answer to this puzzle.

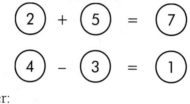

Here is another:

Trick or Treat

Mr. Greensleeve had 13 candies remaining. Note that whether you divide 13 by 2, 3, or by 4, you always get a remainder of 1. It is the only number less than 20 for which that is true.

Donut Try This at Home

Suppose a regular donut has 100 calories. If a low-calorie donut has 95 percent fewer calories, it must have 5 calories. Therefore you must eat 20 low-calorie donuts to get as many calories as you get from one regular donut.

The Long Way Around

The total distance around the diagram is 8 + 15 + 8 + 15 = 46 units. It makes no difference that the upper right portion of the diagram includes a set of "steps." That's because if you pushed out those steps, you could create an 8-by-15 rectangle, and the distance around that rectangle (its "perimeter") would be precisely 46 units.

Starting to Waffle

The stationary machine makes 3 waffles per second. If you had 4 stationary machines, you'd be making 12 waffles per second. The portable machine makes 120 waffles per minute, which is the same as 2 per second. To produce 12 waffles per second you would need 12/2 = 6 portable machines.

A Very Good Year

The next year to have the same property will be 2307: 23 + 07 = 30.

Two Workers Are Better than One

One way to solve the problem is to use fractions. The first worker completes the job in six days, so in one day he will have completed 1/6 of the total. Meanwhile, the second worker would complete 1/12 of the job in one day. Working together, they would complete 1/6 + 1/12 of the job in one day. 1/6 is the same as 2/12, so 2/12 + 1/12 = 3/12, which is the amount of the job they would finish in one day. 3/12 equals 1/4. So together they would complete 1/4 of the job in one day— therefore, it will take them 4 days to get the whole job done!

If you don't want to use fractions, you can do it another way. In twelve days, the first worker would complete the entire job twice, while the second worker would complete it once. Therefore, working together, they would complete three jobs in twelve days, which is a rate of one complete job every four days (12/3 = 4).

An Odd Game of Bingo

23	11	25	15	41
1	37	31	5	17
9	21	FREE	27	47
43	35	33	29	7
19	45	3	39	13

The Price of Fun

The Frisbee costs $3.70 and the softball costs $2.50. As you can see, the Frisbee costs $1.20 more than the softball, and together they cost $6.20.

Fare Wars

The distance that would produce the same fare on both meters is one and a half miles. That's because the Cloud City taxi starts out more expensive by 25 cents. Every quarter-mile, the Megalopolis taxi "makes up" five cents, so everything is even after five quarter-miles. But you can't forget the first quarter-mile, which makes six quarter-miles altogether. That's one and a half miles.

The Powers of Four

Ernie came up with the number 1,048,576. Note that all of Bert's numbers end in 4, while all of Ernie's numbers end in 6. That's all you need to know!

High-Speed Copying

Eight copiers can process 800 sheets in 4 hours. Doubling the number of copiers will double the output without changing the amount of time required.

Divide and Conquer

```
        5 [4]
  9 | 4 [8][6]
   -  [4][5]
          3 [6]
        - [3][6]
          ───────
              0
```

Agent 86

32	19	27	8
10	25	17	34
9	26	18	33
35	16	24	11

Comic Relief

One 10-ruble book, two 2-ruble books, and three 1-ruble books add up to six books and 17 rubles.

A Pane in the Neck

There are 15 panes, each 6 x 10, and it takes 30 seconds to wash a 6 x 10 area, but remember that the windows must be washed on both sides! That means it takes one minute per pane, for a total of 15 minutes. Why didn't Harvey just do it himself and spare everyone the trouble?

Putting Your Two Cents In

The pad could cost 25 cents. Aaron had 23 cents and Bobby had one cent. Together they had 24 cents, which was a penny short.

Surf's Up

The original price of the surfboard was $125. Twenty percent is one-fifth, and one-fifth of 125 is 25. If you subtract $25 from $125, you get $100, which is the sale price of the surfboard.

Apple Picking

They all cost the same!

Ten apples = 1 bag (5¢) plus 3 apples at 15¢ each (45¢) = 50¢

Thirty apples = 4 bags (20¢) plus 2 apples at 15¢ each (30¢)
= 50¢

Fifty apples = 7 bags (35¢) plus 1 apple at 15¢ (15¢) = 50¢

Playing the Triangle

The key to this puzzle is that if you add up the lengths of any two sides of any triangle, the sum must be greater than the third side. Why is this true? Because the shortest distance between any two points is a straight line. For example, in the diagram below, AB + BC could never be less than AC, because then the indirect route from A to C—stopping off at B along the way—would be shorter than the direct route!

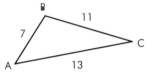

What this means is that 5 cannot be the third side, because 5 + 7 < 13. In the same way, 21 is impossible, because 7 + 13 < 21. That leaves 11 as the only possible answer.

It All Adds Up

The number is 624.

Generation Gap

Grandpa Jones is 78. His four grandchildren are 18, 19, 20, and 21. Note that 18 + 19 + 20 + 21 = 78.
It is not possible for the sum of four consecutive numbers to be equal to 76 or 80. In general, the sum of four consecutive numbers will never be divisible by 4! (Both 76 and 80 *are* divisible by 4.)

The French Connection

One way to compute the average test scores for the two students is to add up their individual test scores and divide by 5.

Average for Sandy = (94+79+84+75+88)/5 = 420/5 = 84

Average for Jason = (72+85+76+81+91)/5 = 405/5 = 81

Sandy has a three point advantage.

An easier way might be to arrange the test scores in the following way:

Sandy: 94 88 84 79 75

Jason: 91 85 81 76 72

It is now easy to see that Sandy has a three-point advantage the whole way through, so her average must be three points higher.

The Long Road

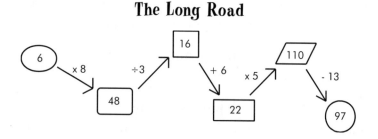

If the Shoe Fits

The total number of shoes is 20,000, the same as the total population of the town. That's because the one-legged people wear one shoe, and, of the remaining people, half wear two shoes and half wear no shoes at all, for an average of one shoe per person.

We Can Work It Out

The total number of dots equals 102. The easiest way is to separate the dots into four rectangles: 3 x 9, 4 x 7, 2 x 11, and 5 x 5. That gives 27 + 28 + 22 + 25 = 102 dots.

Don't Sneeze, Please

Nine hours. The time between the first pill and the fourth pill equals three intervals of three hours each.

Store 24

11 + 11 + 1 + 1 = 24

Thick as a Brick

Here's what the first row of the chimney looks like from above. There are six bricks in this row. Because the chimney consists of five rows, there must be 5 x 6 = 30 bricks altogether.

On All Fours

1 = (4 + 4)/(4 + 4)

2 = (4 x 4)/(4 + 4)

3 = (4 + 4 + 4)/4

4 = 4 + (4 − 4)/4

5 = (4 x 4 + 4)/4

6 = 4 + (4 + 4)/4

7 = 44/4 − 4

8 = 4 + 4 + 4 − 4

9 = 4 + 4 + 4/4

10 = (44 − 4)/4

House of Cards

There are nine cards with a total area of 180, so each one must have an area of 20. The measurements of each card are therefore 4 x 5 (note that 4 x 5 = 20, and that the length of four cards in the diagram is precisely equal to the width of five cards). But if each card is 4 x 5, the height of the figure is nine inches and the length is 20 inches, so the perimeter equals 2 x (20 + 9) = 58 inches.

Once in a Century

There was no parade during the 1970s. The key is to notice that because 11 is just one more than 10, the only way that a sequence of ten numbers can not contain a multiple of eleven is if the very next number is divisible by 11. (This fact was mentioned in the hint for this puzzle.)

With that in mind, one of the numbers 1910, 1920, 1930, etc. must be divisible by 11. The zero doesn't affect anything here, so what we really have is that one of the numbers 191, 192, 193, etc. is divisible by 11. We can see that 198 is the number we're looking for, because 198 = 11 x 18. (Simply add the digits 1 and 8 and put the result in the middle, and you have 11 x 18!!) But if 11 divides evenly into 1980, it also divides evenly into 1969 (180 – 11), but it does not divide evenly into any number in between, which takes care of 1970 through 1979, otherwise known as the seventies!

The Conversion Machine

The only number to stay the number after being put through the conversion machine is the number 40. You can see that 40/5 = 8, 8 x 9 = 72, and 72 − 32 = 40.

In real life, the conversion machine is similar to the transformation between two different temperature scales—the Fahrenheit scale and the Celsius, or Centigrade scale. The difference is that the only temperature to be the same in the Fahrenheit and Celsius scales is 40 degrees *below zero*—when we're too cold to care!

The Easy Way Out

(138 x 109) + (164 x 138) + (138 x 227) = 138 x (109 + 164 + 227) = 138 x 500 = 138 x 1000/2 = 138,000/2 = 69,000.

See You Later, Calculator!

18 percent of 87 equals 87 percent of 18. Technically, 18 percent of 87 equals (18/100) x 87 and 87 percent of 18 equals (87/100) x 18, but you don't have to do any multiplication or division to see that these two expressions are equal, simply because they involve the exact same numbers!

Kangaroo Numbers

The kangaroo numbers on the list are 125 and 912. Note that 125 = 25 x 5, while 912 = 12 x 76.

Blind Date

The answer is your original number. The reason is that the middle number is the *average* of the eight numbers surrounding it—and therefore remains the average of all nine numbers in the 3 x 3 square. If you add up all the numbers surrounding and including 10, for example, you'll get 10 x 9. And dividing by 9 gives you 10, the number you started with.

A Game of Chicken

Two packages of 6, three packages of 9, and three packages of 20 give you (2 x 6) + (3 x 9) + (3 x 20) = 12 + 27 + 60 = 99 McNuggets.

Reel Life Story

There were four senior citizens in the group. They paid $3.00 apiece. The other three adults paid the full price of $6.00 per ticket, for a total of $30.00 for the seven tickets.

Jack in the Box

Suppose you number the cards 1–6, with the jacks being numbers 1 and 2. There are 15 different ways of selecting two cards, as follows:

$$
\begin{array}{ccccc}
1-2 & 2-3 & 3-4 & 4-5 & 5-6 \\
1-3 & 2-4 & 3-5 & 4-6 & \\
1-4 & 2-5 & 3-6 & & \\
1-5 & 2-6 & & & \\
1-6 & & & & \\
\end{array}
$$

Of these 15, only the last three columns don't contain a jack.

There are 6 choices among these three columns, so the chance of not choosing either jack is 6/15, or 2/5. The chance of choosing at least one jack is 3/5, so that is the more likely event.

The Right Stuff

The answer is 43. Simply add up 10 + 65 + 58, getting a total of 133, then subtract 90 to get the answer. The reason this works is that when you add up 10, 65, and 58, you are "double-counting" the people with experience in both sales and publishing (the group you're interested in). So just subtract the original number of applicants (90) and you're left with the experienced people—single-counted, just the way you want!

The Twelve Days of Christmas

The presents that show up the most are those of the sixth and seventh days—the geese a' laying and the swans a' swimming. The six geese are mentioned seven times, for a total of 42, and the seven swans show up six times, again for a total of 42. (The partridge shows up the most frequently, but only one at a time!)

Oh, Brother!

If you take the product of the first eight whole numbers— 8 x 7 x 6 x 5 x 4 x 3 x 2 x 1—and divide by the product of the first six whole numbers—6 x 5 x 4 x 3 x 2 x 1— everything cancels out except the eight and the seven. That means 8!/6! = 8 x 7 = 56.

Numbers on the House

A total of 91 numbers are required—one each for the nine houses numbered 1–9, and two each for the houses numbered 10–50.

Of these 91, each of the numbers 1–4 is used 15 times, the number 5 is used 6 times, and each of the numbers 6, 7, 8, 9, and 0 is used 5 times. Sure enough, (4 x 15) + 6 + (5 x 5) = 60 + 6 + 25 = 91.

Square Feet

There were 81 soldiers originally, marching in a 9 x 9 square. After 32 of them were called away, that left 49 soldiers, who then marched in a 7 x 7 square.

If not for the fact that there are at least eight soldiers in the second square, there would have been a second solution: with 36 soldiers originally and 32 called away. Then you would have been left with 4, another perfect square!

Incomplete Sentences

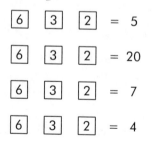

He Was Framed!

As long as you didn't answer too fast, this one wasn't all that tough. The width of the picture frame was 1/2 of an inch. The trick is not to answer one inch— remember, the frame goes around all four sides of the picture!

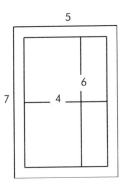

Double Trouble

5 8 × 3 = 1 7 4 = 2 9 × 6

Misery Loves Company

Jones did worse than Smith, even after Smith's second 60% loss. To see why, assume that each man started with $1,000, as suggested in the hint. Then Jones ended up with $150, following his 85% loss. Smith had $400 after his first loss. After his second loss he had $400 − (60% of $400). But 60% of $400 equals $240, so he ended up with $400 − $240 = $160, barely better than Jones. The key is that Smith's second 60% loss was made on a smaller investment—$400 versus $1,000.

Strange but True

The numbers are 1, 2, and 3. It's easy to check that $1 + 2 + 3 = 1 \times 2 \times 3 = 6$.

Say the Magic Words

The values of the magic words are as follows:
ABRACADABRA = 1 + 2 + 18 + 1 + 3 + 1 + 4 + 1 + 2 + 18 + 1
    = 52
PRESTO = 16 + 18 + 5 + 19 + 20 + 15 = 93
SHAZAM = 19 + 8 + 1 + 26 + 1 + 13 = 68
As you can see, PRESTO has the highest value. And even though ABRACADABRA is the longest word by far, it has the lowest value.

A Famous Triangle

The sum of the elements of the seventh row equals 64. To get this total, you have two choices. One is to figure out the elements of the seventh row and add them all up. The other thing you can do is notice the pattern of the earlier rows. You can see that the pattern, starting with the second row, goes 2, 4, 8, 16, and so on—each new row doubles the result of the row before! Continuing all the way to the seventh row, we get the same answer: 64.

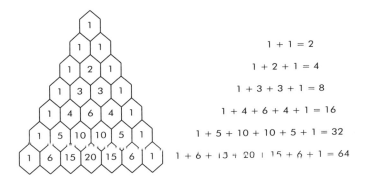

$$1 + 1 = 2$$
$$1 + 2 + 1 = 4$$
$$1 + 3 + 3 + 1 = 8$$
$$1 + 4 + 6 + 4 + 1 = 16$$
$$1 + 5 + 10 + 10 + 5 + 1 = 32$$
$$1 + 6 + 15 + 20 + 15 + 6 + 1 = 64$$

Follow the Directions

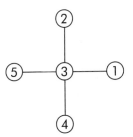

The middle number could be 3, which of course is also the middle number of 1, 2, 3, 4, and 5. The idea is that you can pair the 1 and 5 to give you a 6, and you can pair the 2 and 4 to give you another 6. The sum in any direction is 9. (There are four answers with this number arrangement, obtained by switching the positions of the 5 and 1 or the 4 and 2.) Can you think of any other solutions with a 3 not in the middle?

Letter Logic

G must stand for 1, because a three-digit number plus a two-digit number cannot be possibly be greater than 1,000. Similarly, the E must stand for 9, because if it were anything less than 9, it couldn't carry over to four digits after adding a two-digit number. We also know that A must equal 0, for similar reasons. But we have D + 1 = 9, so D = 8. The last step is the middle column, but the only way to get a sum of 10 or greater (to produce the carrying in the leftmost column) without repeating letters is to have N = 7 and M = 2.

$$\begin{array}{r} 978 \\ + \ 51 \\ \hline 1029 \end{array}$$

Miles to Go

The gap between the two odometers is 445 miles, a gap that will not change. Therefore, the main odometer will be twice the trip odometer when the trip odometer reads 445 miles. That will happen in precisely 445 − 22 = 423 miles.

Slippery Slopes

Ten days. After 9 days and 9 nights, she is at 9000 feet. On the 10th day she climbs 3000 feet to the summit!

The Long and the Short of the Grass

They mowed the grass on 9 Saturdays, earning 9 x $2 = $18, and missed 6 Saturdays, losing 6 x $3 = $18.

Potato Pairs

Add all the weights together and divide by two to get the total weight of the three potatoes: (3+5+4)/2 = 6 pounds. Now, since A and B together weigh 3 pounds, and A + B + C together weigh 6 pounds, then C must weigh 3 pounds. A and C together weigh 5 pounds, which means that A must weigh 2 pounds; so Cal should buy either A and B or A and C.

Crackers!

This is surprisingly easy; the trick is to add a plain cracker. Then Marty has a choice of 2—mayo or plain. Marty and Jake have a choice of 4; when Hank arrives they have a choice of 8, since the number of choices doubles with each new person. So when Hank comes there will be 16 choices—or 15 spreads. When Charlie is there they'll have 32 choices—31 spreads. And Fred will bring the total to 64 choices—63 spreads!

Witches' Brew

The pan holds 3 pints; fill it and then fill the jug from it. The jug holds 1 pint; so that leaves exactly 2 pints in the pan. Pour it into the cauldron and carry on cooking!

Witches' Stew

Fill the pitcher to the brim. Use it to fill the pot, which leaves just 2 pints in the pitcher. Empty the pot back into the bucket. Pour the 2 pints from the pitcher into the pot. Fill the pitcher again. Now carefully top off the pot from the pitcher. This will take exactly 1 pint, because there are 2 pints in it already. That leaves exactly 4 pints in the pitcher—pour them into the cauldron!

Cyclomania

Donna saw more than one tricycle; so at least six of the wheels must have belonged to tricycles. Suppose there had been three tricycles; then they would have had 9 wheels, which would have left only 3 wheels—not enough for more than one bicycle. So there must have been exactly two tricycles. That makes 6 wheels; so the other 6 wheels must have belonged to bikes; therefore there must have been 3 bikes and 2 trikes.

Cookie Jars

Joe has no cookies; so this puzzle is easy. If Ken gave him one, he'd have a total of one; so if they have the same number, Ken must also have one left. Therefore Ken must have two to begin with.

Spring Flowers

The way to figure this out is to start at the end with 39 petals, and remember that the primroses must provide either 5 petals or 10 or 15 or 20 or 25 or 30 or 35—a multiple of 5. Now suppose there was only one celandine (8 petals); that would leave 31 petals (39 − 8 = 31). The rest can't be primroses, because 31 is not an exact multiple of 5. Suppose there were two celandines; that would make 16 petals, leaving 23. No good! Three celandines = 24 petals, and 39 − 24 = 15 petals. Bingo! The answer must be 3 celandines and 3 primroses.

Check: 3 x 8 = 24 and 3 x 5 = 15, and 24 + 15 = 39. So Rose is (3+3), or 6.

Fleabags
Captain has two fleas; Champ has four.

Squares & Cubes
64 = 8 x 8 and 4 x 4 x 4

Cubes & Squares
The only number between 100 and 999 that is both a square and a cube is 729, which is 27 x 27 and 9 x 9 x 9.

Old MacDonald
All the 12 wings must have belonged to turkeys, because pigs don't usually have any; so he must have had 6 turkeys (with 2 wings each). The 6 turkeys must have had 12 legs; leaving 12 legs for the pigs, and since each pig has 4 legs, that makes 3 pigs. So Old MacDonald had 3 pigs and 6 turkeys.

LoadsaLegs
One had 6 legs; the other had 10.

Pyramids
Susie needs 56 cookies; Ben needs 55.

Wrong Envelope?
Think of the three envelopes as A, B, and C, and the three

letters as a, b, and c. Then you can write down the six
different ways of arranging the letters like this:

1	2	3	4	5	6
Aa	**Aa**	Ab	Ab	Ac	Ac
Bb	Bc	Ba	Bc	Ba	**Bb**
Cc	Cb	**Cc**	Ca	Cb	Ca

Only #1 has all the letters in the right envelopes; so there are
five ways of putting at least one letter into the wrong
envelope, and your chance of getting it all right just by luck is
one in six.

There are only two arrangements with all the letters in the
wrong envelopes. Can you find any arrangements with two
letters in the right envelopes and one wrong?

Train Crash

In the hour before the crash one train must have traveled 25
miles, and the other 15. So one hour before the crash they
were (25 + 15) or 40 miles apart.

Squished Fly

The trains traveled for exactly one hour before they crashed.
So at 50 mph, the fly must have flown exactly 50 miles.

Heavybrix

If a brick weighs a pound and a half a brick, then two bricks weigh 2 pounds and a brick.

So taking a brick away from each side, one brick weighs 2 pounds. So two bricks weigh 4 pounds.

 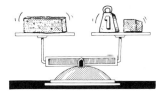

Object Puzzle Answers

Line Bogglers

Two-Way Street

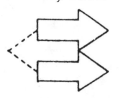

Sum Time

6 + 5 = 9???

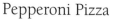
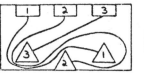

In Need of Repair

1 4 3 + 5 = 148
1 + 3 + 5 ≠ 148

Tunnels

Pepperoni Pizza

Pencil Puzzles

1.

2.

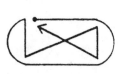

3.

4.

5.

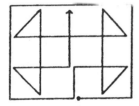

6.

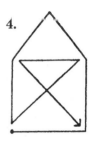

7.

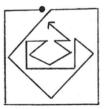

8.

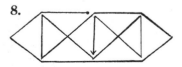

Toothpick Teasers

Architect

Crisscross

Aquarium

Square Deal

In and Out

Equilateral Triangles

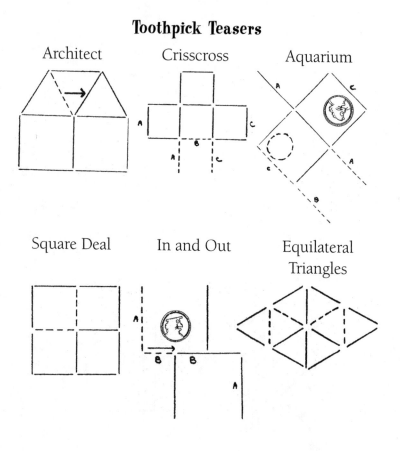

Coin Bafflers

Over Easy

Four Across

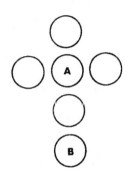

Place coin B on coin A.

Do Not Touch

You can remove the coin from the glass by just turning the page a third of a turn to the right.

Constellation

2 to 7

8 to 5 to 2

6 to 3 to 8 to 5

4 to 1 to 6 to 3 to 8

7 to 4 to 1 to 6

2 to 7 to 4

5 to 2

Coin Checkers

1. Slide H (heads) into empty space.

2. Jump H with a T (tails).

3. Slide T into new empty space.

4. Jump T with an H.

5. Jump other T with other H.

6. Slide T into empty space.

7. Jump H with a T.

8. Slide H just jumped into empty space.

Number Juggling

Box Score

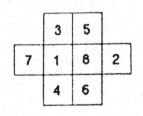

Wheel Numbers

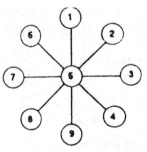

Bermuda Triangle

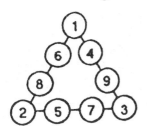

Troublesum

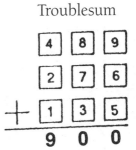

Magic Square

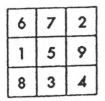

Hexagram

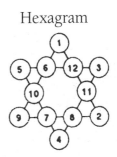

Riddle Me

It depends on how many kids are playing in the yard at the time!

Riddle Me II

Because the nickel has more cents (sense)!

Brain Busters

Stargazer

Box Score II

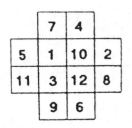

Windowpanes

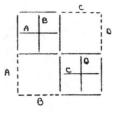

Dot to Dot

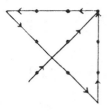

Tunnels II
One possible solution:

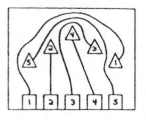

Tetrahedron

CALCULATOR RIDDLES

1. A hole. When you take away more dirt, the hole gets larger!

2. A goose. A goose has 2 legs but no goose has 4 legs.

3. Ellie. They are her parents, so she must be one of their children!

4. 16 legs (the decimal point separates numbers and words). One of the four singers is a *tenor* and 10 + 2 + 2 + 2 = 16!

5. 9 eels, because 9 eels were *not* sold!

6. Lee, the butcher. He weighs meat all day long!

7. 1 h (hour). The third pill will be taken 1 hour after the first pill!

8. ($) 100 bill. It is worth $99 more than the new one ($1)!

9. Bob scored higher on the math test because glasses improve di *vision*!

10. 12s (seconds). January second, February 2, March second, etc.!

11. Holes, so 75 kilograms of water leaked out!

12. Leslie. She was more exhausted because of all the numbers that she had to carry!

    Bill, because of all the borrowing that he had to do! Bess, because she was so *productive*!

13. 2. The math teacher brought the student to!

14. A googol. It has 101 digits!

15. His boss is right. *All* of the months have at least 28 days!

16. 8.9 (seven ate nine)!

17. The number 5,317. It *lies* when it is resting on its back!

18. 0. No matter how you turn the calculator, there is no dirt in a hole!

19. 2 eggs. You took 2 eggs so you *have* 2 eggs!

20. His legs, because he puts down 3 and carries 1!

Index

WHAT IS MENSA?

Mensa—The High IQ Society

Mensa is the international society for people with a high IQ. We have more than 100,000 members in over 40 countries worldwide.

The society's aims are:
- to identify and foster human intelligence for the benefit of humanity;
- to encourage research in the nature, characteristics, and uses of intelligence;
- to provide a stimulating intellectual and social environment for its members.

Anyone with an IQ score in the top two percent of the population is eligible to become a member of Mensa—are you the "one in 50" we've been looking for?

Mensa membership offers an excellent range of benefits:
- Networking and social activities nationally and around the world;
- Special Interest Groups (hundreds of chances to pursue your hobbies and interests—from art to zoology!);
- Monthly International Journal, national magazines, and regional newsletters;
- Local meetings—from game challenges to food and drink;
- National and international weekend gatherings and conferences;
- Intellectually stimulating lectures and seminars;
- Access to the worldwide SIGHT network for travelers and hosts.

**For more information about
Mensa International:**

www.mensa.org
Mensa International
15 The Ivories
6–8 Northampton Street
Islington, London N1 2HY
United Kingdom

**For more information about
American Mensa:**

www.us.mensa.org
Telephone: (800) 66-MENSA
American Mensa Ltd.
1229 Corporate Drive West
Arlington, TX 76006-6103 US

**For more information about
British Mensa (UK and Ireland):**

www.mensa.org.uk
Telephone: +44 (0) 1902 772771
E-mail: enquiries@mensa.org.uk
British Mensa Ltd.
St. John's House
St. John's Square
Wolverhampton WV2 4AH
United Kingdom